Anonymous

Prayers for the sick chamber

Anonymous
Prayers for the sick chamber
ISBN/EAN: 9783337283988
Printed in Europe, USA, Canada, Australia, Japan
Cover: Foto ©Lupo / pixelio.de

More available books at **www.hansebooks.com**

PRAYERS

FOR

THE SICK CHAMBER

STRAHAN AND CO., PUBLISHERS
139 GRAND STREET, NEW YORK
1867

TO

ALL THE SICK AND DYING,

TO THOSE WHO HAVE LEARNED ONLY THE TRIALS OF SICKNESS.

TO THOSE WHO HAVE ALSO TASTED OF THE BLESSINGS OF SICKNESS.

THIS LITTLE BOOK

IS AFFECTIONATELY DEDICATED,

IN THE EARNEST HOPE

THAT IT MAY LEAD THEM YET MORE TO THE ONLY

BOOK

IN WHICH "EVERY WORD IS PURE,"

AND WHICH CAN ALONE STRENGTHEN,

AND SOOTHE, AND COMFORT,

IN LONG SICKNESS,

AND IN THE DYING HOUR.

CONTENTS.

PAGE

A Few Words about the Difficulties of Prayer in Sickness and in Weakness 1

PART I.—FOR THE SICK.

PRAYERS.

For the Morning	27
For the Evening	31
For Midnight	34
For Repentance	37
For Sorrow for Sin	38
For Forgiveness of Sin	40
For Faith in the Lord Jesus Christ . . .	41
For Patience	44
For Contentment	46
*For calmness of Mind	49
For Humility	51
For Rest in God in Weakness	53
For those in Pain	55
*For those in Infirmities which humiliate . .	57

CONTENTS.

	PAGE
For those suffering from Hunger	60
For those suffering from Thirst	62
For those in Poverty	65
For those in Loneliness	69
*For those in confirmed long Illness	71
*For those in uncertainty as to the Length and Termination of Illness	74
*For those in prospect of an inactive Life; against Impatience and Self-will	76
*For help in Delirium	79
For help in Restlessness	81
*For those in prospect of an Operation	84
For those in great Weakness	86
For those in great Weakness and inability to Pray	88
For those in great Sickness	91
For those in sore Trouble	93
For those who are very Ill	95
For those who have given way to Irritability	97
For those who are walking in Darkness	99
For those who have forgotten God in time of Health	101
For the Backslider in heart	104
For those who fear they have been deceived	107
For those who are suffering from Wanderings of Mind in Weakness	109
For those who feel the Difficulty of Prayer in Weakness	112
For those who have been taken up by the Cares of this Life, and been over-anxious	114
*For those who complain of want of Sympathy	116
*That suffering may not produce Selfishness	119
For the Aged	121
For one afflicted with Blindness	124
For one afflicted with Deafness	126
In wearisome Nights	129
On Sundays	130

CONTENTS.

PAGE

*Prayer for a Blessing on the use of Medicine, and other remedies 133
*That sickness may bring forth its proper Fruits . . 135
To be enabled to give thanks for Suffering . . . 137
That the purpose of Suffering may be fulfilled in us, which is to liken us to Christ 140
For those who believe that Death is coming near and desire it, but are told that it is far distant . . 143
For those who are recovering from Sickness, and have the prospect of returning to active Life . . 147
Before receiving the Sacrament of the Lord's Supper . 151

INTERCESSIONS.

For the Church and Clergy 154
For Friends who are with us, and for those who are absent, and for Nurses and Attendants . . 157
*For Medical men 161

THANKSGIVINGS.

*For Friends 164
*For bodily Comforts 166
*For spiritual Consolations 168
*For Sickness 171
*For Sorrow 173
*For our Baptismal Inheritance 176

PART II.—FOR THE DYING.

PRAYERS.

In the prospect of Death 181
For those who have a fear of Death 182

	PAGE
When Death is very near	185
For those who have a desire to depart, but are willing to wait the appointed time	187
For those of our Family and Friends who will be left at our Death	189
About the Resurrection of the Body, and the great comfort to be derived from it	192

THANKSGIVINGS.

*For Death	196
For the Joys of Heaven	198

Verses from Holy Scripture, and Prayers suitable to be read to dying Persons by their Friends	203

The Prayers marked thus * were supplied by a sick and suffering Friend.

A

FEW WORDS

ABOUT

THE DIFFICULTIES OF PRAYER

IN SICKNESS AND IN WEAKNESS.

AMONGST the many trials which sickness brings, there is one which seems to be the portion of all who are sick and suffering, however varied their circumstances. There are perhaps very few who have been long ill, and brought into weakness, who do not find that some of their greatest trials arise out of their difficulties about prayer.

The more earnest-minded they are, the more they have set their affections on things above, the sadder these lets and hindrances will be to them; each one thinks that he " mourns apart;" that he alone suffers from this sorrow; that it is his own fault and great sin; and that no one else can be so troubled by such difficulties, and coldnesses, and hindrances.

But if it is the heritage of all who are sick and weak, there surely must be some purpose and meaning in it, and some remedy for it; not one indeed which will bring instant cure, but which the oftener it is tried, the more sure its effect will be.

Perhaps the mistaken ideas people commonly have about sickness, is one cause of this trial; it is often looked upon as a state set apart, one in which every thing is favorable "to the attainment of everlasting life;" in which worldly things assume their true places, and are cast into the shade, and in which prayer becomes the chief work of their lives. People in health often speak to the sick as if it was the work given them to do, and which they could do then as never before; they think that the sick have so much time and so few distractions. How often such words fall like lead upon the hearts of the sick, who feel that therein lies their greatest conflict, their deepest trial; alas! they well know that their distractions are great, and the time left by sickness and all its appliances very little, and that little, how often it is mere endurance—a passive state. Their trials are not less than in the days of health, but they are altogether different, and when first a long sickness comes, the change is so great that the mere getting accustomed to it, seems work enough, and beyond their strength.

In short, sharp illnesses, there is often a great deal of enjoyment of spiritual things, and the time seems to be set apart as a holy thing, in which to review the past and prepare again for the battle of life; but in long sickness the case is generally very different, for the mind becomes worn and weakened by suffering, and sometimes as the strength fails this trial becomes greater.

Some of the personal sting of it would be taken away, if we believed it was the appointed lot of all the sick; instead of feeling it a hard and lonely trial, we should learn to feel for all our fellow-sufferers, and in sympathy with them should lose ourselves, and the constant dwelling upon this as a personal and solitary grief. There must be a meaning and a wise purpose in it; the God of love would not send it to all the large family of the sick and the weak, unless there were a " needs be" that they should be " in heaviness."

In health, perhaps, even prayer may have become too mechanical; the same hours, the same posture, the same circumstances, and this seemed enough. Sickness and weakness change all this; the inability to kneel, or to change the posture to one of devotion, is doubtless a great hindrance, and, if it is not watched against, will be more so; but as a remedy against this, some posture may surely be set apart, even in bed, which may help to recollection; carefully avoiding any that might minister to sleep; because one of the great trials about prayer in sickness is, the tendency to drowsiness; few distresses are greater than to find how quickly prayer has ended in sleep, but if it has been watched against and resisted, it is no sin, only a trial which is to "humble us and do us good."

Another cause is the monotony of a sick life; the fewness of its variations tell on the mind by degrees; sometimes producing discouragement, at other times indifference, or to some people, irritability.

Then the idea that there will not be interruptions, and that another time when we feel a little stronger will be better for prayer, is one of the forms of the temptation, and is the best resisted by having stated times for everything. Sick people greatly need the help of time and seasons; each one must make the rule for himself, and the more closely he is able to keep to it, the better for him. In this, the habits acquired in days of health will much affect the days of sickness; those who have yielded to desultory habits in other days, will find the punishment now: just as in common things, sick people will find that if they have not yielded to indolence in days of health, the difficulty will be far less in sickness of rousing themselves to exertion, and putting forth the little strength they have for the common duties of life, which others give up and let the habits of sickness grow fast upon them. It is true that the latter receive more sympathy, and are thought more ill, and thus they have their reward, but not the same blessing. So likewise those who have accustomed themselves to subdue the outward expression of pain and suffering, may indeed be often mistaken here upon earth, but they spare their friends much sorrow and pain, and they have the great blessing of learning, by that means, to lie still in the hands of God.

Another of the difficulties about prayer arises from the irritability of the nerves; much of this, doubtless, depends on the nature of the disease and on the medicines taken, but in all cases of long sickness there must be more or less of it. But this is not *sin* but *suffering;* if it be so resisted that the outward expression of it is overcome, it is all that can be looked for, and "with such sacrifices God is well pleased." To judge by this would be very false, for while some diseases and some remedies may so irritate the nerves, as to make all continuous thought impossible, the effect may be just the reverse in many cases, and excited and pleasant feelings may be produced in prayer. We should beware of mistaking these for realities, or of trusting to any kind of feelings as tests of the spiritual state.

One of the greatest trials arising out of weakness of body, is the impossibility of fixing the mind steadily on holy things. Often the pain is very great which is caused by such efforts, so great as to prevent the very thing which we desire to attain. And then comes the self-reproach—and how bitter that is! Because the mind seems capable only of light and frivolous thoughts, and will tease and trouble itself about trifling matters; these we seem to dwell on; they magnify themselves, shaping themselves often, until they seem to become things of importance. At other times we feel that they are trifles, yet they flit before us and seem to constrain our attention. Perhaps it is something we may have heard long ago, and then heeded not; or something that we think we never heard; or some person comes before our minds, and will not go away; or some name teases us that we cannot catch; or some face that we cannot remember; or something too silly almost to tell to ourselves. Sick people must take into account, however, that this is not the case *only* at their prayers; it is frequently besides, especially in sleep, when we surely cannot help it: how what has happened in the day haunts us then; how people seem to stand around our bed and will not go away. We must not struggle too hard against this trial; it is not the way to overcome it. The grasp of our minds is much smaller than in the days of health; we must not try to go beyond it; violent efforts exhaust the strength and increase the evil. It is better not to go on too long in fighting against such thoughts. To repeat a short Psalm is far better; and if we go on repeating the same, it is less effort than taking more than one, and better keeps out the thoughts which trouble us. Or a hymn may be repeated in the same manner. Thus by degrees the wandering thoughts may pass away, and we may turn those words of Holy Scripture into prayer, taking a verse at a time and meditating upon it. But even that must not last too long whilst we are so weak. It is of no use in such states trying to go on with prayer (if by that is meant saying *words* to God), and trying thereby to overcome wanderings; it only increases the evil, and leaves us more weak, and sad, and depressed, than when we began. Perhaps it may be objected, that to say the same words again and again would be vain repetition. Yet it is written, that in that last night of the agony of our Lord in the garden, He thrice returned, saying the same words, "Father, if it be possible, let this cup pass from me." We may say the same words, if we be content to receive the same answer which St. Paul received, when he "besought the Lord thrice," that the thorn in the flesh might be taken from Him: his prayer was answered; not as he then wished, but in a far higher way, "My grace is sufficient for thee." And it is sufficient for every sick person still, and ever will be.

One more hindrance to prayer may be mentioned—the much stronger hold which the things that are *seen* have upon us. We are always seeking for something *visible;* but the "things which are seen are temporal, and the things which are not seen are eternal." How little idea we have of that which is unseen or eternal! And we sometimes feel as if our prayers went no where, because we do not see the result of them.

Is there nothing of self in the wish to pray well? Should we not think our souls in a better state if we could? And would not that please *us* rather than be pleasing to God? Self is the hindrance to prayer, it comes between God and the soul. We wish for *pleasure* even in our devotions; our Father sees that we need *discipline*, and this is a very needful part of our training. It is thus we learn to "refrain our souls and keep them low." We should never learn to put our full trust and confidence only in His mercy without it. To go on and persevere, amidst discouragements, is a far higher service, and greater test of sincerity, than any other we could have been called on to make. When we suppose that God requires of us more than He has given us the power to perform, we make Him a "hard Master, reaping where He has not sown, and gathering where He has not strawed,"—a *task-master*, not a loving Father. He has set us our task now, and we find it a very hard one, for it is to lie still; but if we go beyond what He has set us, we are not "doing our duty in that state of life unto which it has pleased God to call us;" it is only in "quietness and confidence" that we can "possess our strength." For every talent which He has given us, we shall surely have to give account; but the talents which He has either *not* given us, or has taken away from us, are not ours; we have no business with them. It is quite enough for us to improve what are given to us; He knows what He has given; He knows what He has taken away; and He is a "righteous Judge," strong and patient. What has been said of prayer applies equally to reading the Scriptures. He knows what we can, and what we cannot do; it may be more effort to read a single verse at one time, than many chapters at another. Only let us do what we can, and leave the rest to God. We often think that too much depends on our prayers. If we never think that our salvation depends on them, at any rate, we think that everything short of it does; alas! if it did, what hope would there be for any of us? But do our prayers bring Christ nearer to us? Is it not that He is thereby drawing us to Him? "He dwelleth with us, and shall be in us." It is His intercession which gives worthiness to our prayers; He sifts them, and does not offer for us the many foolish petitions which would be for the ruin of our souls if they were answered as we wish, and ask that they should be. We "lay the gift on the altar;" it is He who offers it up. To think of our prayers, and what they work out for us, is after all looking *to* ourselves: looking *from* Christ. But is there so great a contrast between our prayers now in sickness, and what they were in days of health? Were they so very fervent then? Did we never complain of wandering thoughts then? And yet we had not the same excuse that we now have. They were more continuous and regular, perhaps, but were they more earnest? Were they such as they ought to have been, and as we now suppose that they were?

It is earnestness, reality, simplicity, and sincerity, not length, not the going through certain subjects regularly that constitutes prayer: some of the most earnest prayers that were ever offered, and that were the most quickly answered, contained very few words, "Lord, save me, or I perish." "Jesus, Thou Son of David, have mercy upon me." "Lord, I believe, help Thou mine unbelief." "Lord, remember me, when Thou comest into thy kingdom." The cry of a drowning man would be very brief and unstudied, but full of earnestness and purpose, and would be in such a case fuller of meaning, and gain more immediate attention, than if he spoke many long sentences at another time. O that sickness might teach any of us to be *as* earnest, *as* real, *as* simple! for if sickness teaches us to pray with full purpose of heart, however briefly, it will not have come to us in vain. How often we have asked to be taught to pray. Perhaps this sickness is the answer. We are to be taught, by having everything wherein we trusted taken away from us, and till then we shall not be brought into entire dependence upon God. It is very painful to feel that almost every prayer (at any rate for a time) is to be a trial, and not an enjoyment as we would fain have it: but it is most wholesome discipline, and we shall surely reap the benefit of it another day. It is our " Father's loving correction." It is good for us to have our prayers, and everything else in which we have trusted, broken to pieces; that " the Lord alone may be exalted in that day." And this sickness is the day of His visitation, the " hand of God hath touched " us. Let us give hearty thanks to Him, for this and all blessings.

If prayer is converse with God, what does that mean ? Does it need words ? He can hear the " voice of our breathing;" therefore we need not " strive nor cry, nor lift up our voice," for He is very near to us, strengthening us and upholding us with the right hand of His righteousness.

If a little child wanted his earthly father to do something for him, would he ask it in many or formal words? And shall we treat our Heavenly Father, who is "very pitiful and of tender mercy," with *less* trust and confidence? Even with earthly parents, it is the *intention* of the child that they look at, or desire to discover. They would not charge it with sin, and punish it for every mistake or folly. How much more, then, must He who "searcheth the heart," and knows all our thoughts, look at our intention? He sees the heart—He reads it: if He sees that we desire to pray, but that weakness hinders, He accepts the intention, and "like as a father pitieth his children, so doth the Lord pity them that fear Him, for He knoweth our frame, He remembereth that we are dust;" He will "not impute iniquity to us."

Let us always strive to look at all these difficulties about prayer as *trials*, as meant to be so by our most loving Father, who Himself has sent them to us. Let us believe in His love, and rest in that alone. Let us be sure that He understands us even before we try to express our wants to Him; and that He has "loved us with an everlasting love, and therefore with loving-kindness has He drawn" us nearer to Himself by the very discipline that we shrink from. We need not wait, therefore, till we can say long prayers. Short prayers are great helps, and are especially necessary in sharp pain or great weakness. They often save from dangers; for these are times of peculiar temptation: "Lord, help me;"—"My Father, this is a time of need, and I come to Thee to help me;"—"Lord, hear my crying." Such words have helped many sufferers, and enabled them to lie down and rest in His arms, who is always close at hand to help, support, strengthen, and comfort. Let us be careful never to resist emotions to prayer; it may be that by doing so we grieve the Spirit of God—certainly we deprive our own souls of blessing.

And now of what we have said this is

the sum. The only true remedy against these trying difficulties about prayer, is to rest in the love of God. The more we are enabled to do so, the more we shall know of that "peace which passeth all understanding:" it will "keep our hearts and minds," and we shall find how true it is that the world can neither give nor take it away. If "the love of God were shed abroad in our hearts by the Holy Ghost," all things else would be to us as dross; and we should "determine to know nothing but Christ and Him crucified." Then we should know that prayer is worship: that worship, to be acceptable, must be offered according to the will of God; so that if He sends us sickness, we are to worship Him by the entire resignation of ourselves, by the offering up of our bodies as a "living sacrifice"—offering them to suffer as He sees necessary for us, to be laid as low as He wills, to lose our will in His will. Silence and submission to the will of God is the service required of us now; and by God's grace this may become the purest and the holiest offering that we ever had to bring. There may have been much of self in our former attempts at sacrifice; but in this, if we will only let God work in us without any resistance on our parts, it cannot be so. But let us "do all things without murmurings and disputings." Let us resign our wills, without complaining to our fellow-creatures, or telling them how hard it is for us to do so. The less we struggle, the easier it will be—"Woe to him who striveth against his Maker." If we murmur, we shall rob ourselves of the blessing which this trial surely contains; it may seem to come in a strange guise, yet may bring us a message from the God of love. We must, however, be patient. Resting in God and in His perfect love is not a lesson learnt in an hour or a day, but the gradual work of our lives. We must be patient with ourselves, and not get out of heart because we learn it so slowly, and often seem to forget it again. We must be patient with our Teacher, who never grows weary of teaching us: His lessons are all taught in perfect wisdom; they often seem to us as if they would work out just the wrong thing; but He knows what He is doing, and "with Him is no variableness, neither shadow of turning." He will "work all His works in us."

Let us not be discouraged because our memories fail, and we can remember nothing good, as it seems to us; but let us always take comfort in the promise, that the "Holy Ghost will take of the things of Christ, and show them unto us;" and that He "will bring all things to our remembrance, whatsoever Christ hath spoken" to us, and the rest had far better be forgotten.

How great the comfort is that the "Holy Ghost maketh intercession for us with groanings which cannot be uttered." We know not what to pray for as we ought, but He "helpeth our infirmities," and "puts into our minds good desires."

And we "have a merciful and faithful High Priest, who maketh reconciliation for the sins of the people;" "wherefore He is able to save them to the uttermost that come unto God by Him, seeing He ever liveth to make intercession for them." What more do we need? Only this,—to cease from ourselves, and to depend wholly upon Christ; to believe that "all our prayers are nothing worth;" that their worthiness comes only through His intercession. Let us go forward then, and be no more "discouraged because of the way." Yet a little while, and all discouragement shall be ended, and "God shall wipe away all tears from our eyes," and "in His light we shall see light."

Amongst the sick there are many, probably, who never learnt the blessing of prayer, until they were taught by sickness to turn to the God of love as their Father, and to the Lord Jesus as their only Saviour. If they said their prayers in the days of health, they did not heed the wandering thoughts; prayer was with them a habit, a formal thing. But when their ears were opened to hear the voice of God, and they awoke as from a sleep, and first tried to pray, they found the task very difficult; they longed to pray, they felt the need of it in earnest; but their minds seemed to be fixed on nothing. This is a sore distress; but the remedy is the same for them—to rest in the love of God, and not to be over anxious about the words spoken in prayer, their number or their fervency. Our Father, " of His great and endless pity," has taught you to seek Him. He would not have done so if He had not loved you, and willed your salvation. But He does not expect of you what He does of those who have long been seeking Him: the cry of a child as really shows life as the voice of a man. A child learning to speak has few words, perhaps but one at first; but by degrees he gets more and more. Thus it is with you; and if you have no words, the Lord's Prayer will express all your needs for you. Do not say to anything that you may read here, "it is high, I cannot attain to it." You are not called to do so yet. The simpler prayer is, the truer it is. It is better not to question what is prayer and what is not. It is enough to know that we may tell every thought of our hearts in the most simple words to our Heavenly Father, and that He will hear and understand them: "He will be very gracious unto the voice of thy cry, and when He shall hear it, He will answer thee." "He that hath begun a good work in you will perform it." And if words fail you, He can understand your heart, and see its desire. Only be in earnest, and you shall want no good thing.

May we all who are sick and dying, pray the more earnestly for all who are sick and dying, "remembering those who are in bonds, as bound with them."

"The grace of our Lord Jesus Christ be with us all." Amen.

NOTE TO THE SECOND EDITION.

Since the first edition of these Prayers was published, it has been found that to some sick persons the inverted commas proved a distraction to their eyes when they desired to be unconscious that they were reading. They have therefore been uniformly omitted in this edition.

For the same reason no references have been given, or italics used: there are, however, few sentences which have not been taken partly or entirely from Holy Scripture, or from the Prayer Book.

PART I.

PRAYERS FOR THE SICK.

He Himself bare our sicknesses.

PRAYERS FOR THE SICK.

I.

MORNING.

O LORD, I thank Thee that the night is ended and that the sun has risen again upon the earth. May the Sun of Righteousness arise upon me with healing in His wings. Help me to give Thee hearty thanks that soon there shall be no more night, but that Thou wilt be my everlasting light, and sorrow and sighing shall flee away. Thanks be unto Thee for all Thine unspeakable gifts! Vouchsafe, O Lord, to keep me this day without sin; have mercy upon me, for I am weak; leave me not, neither forsake me. I am sore let and hindered in running the race which Thou hast appointed for me; yet, O Lord, save Thy servant, for I put my trust in Thee. Send me help from Thy holy place, and do Thou mightily defend me. Let the enemy have no advantage over me to-day, nor let the wicked approach to hurt me. Be unto me, O Lord, a strong tower from the face of the enemy. Thou hast brought me into sickness, and I know not when Thou wilt bring me unto death. Help me always to watch, for I know not at what hour Thou wilt come; may I be found ready whenever Thou dost call me. O Lord, I know not what lies before me to-day; but Thou knowest. Thy compassions fail not, they are new every morning: help me to lean on Thee alone; let me take hold of the arm of Thy strength, and be at peace with Thee. I know, O Lord, that Thy judgments are right; let me not be afraid of them. Yet, O my Father, I fear myself; sin is ever present with me; even my very sickness, which Thou hast sent to do me good, tempts me to sin. Draw nigh unto my soul and save it, because of mine enemies. O cleanse Thou me from my secret faults; keep back Thy servant from presumptuous sins, lest they get the dominion over me.

Let the words of my mouth and the meditation of my heart be acceptable in Thy sight to-day. Set a watch, O Lord, on the door of my lips, lest I sin against Thee. Keep me from speaking any hasty, or unkind, or sinful words; keep me from impatience, from murmuring thoughts; from ingratitude or unkindness to others, by word or deed; from want of love and want of sympathy to those about me. Keep me from selfishness, from discontent, from wishing to have things otherwise than Thou hast appointed them. From indolence and self-indulgence, from needless anxieties, from tormenting my mind with trifles, from over-estimation of my trials, from all falseness of mind and of doctrine, good

Lord, deliver me. Give me humility, gentleness, and meekness; help me to give thanks for all Thy gifts, especially for Thy love to me, and for the love which Thou hast put into the hearts of others towards me. Put into my mind good desires, and fill my heart this day with holy thoughts. Let me count these light afflictions as but for a moment, and may I look not at the things which are seen, and are temporal, but at the things which are unseen, and eternal. Bless those who govern this country. Give Thy heavenly blessing to the Church and the Clergy, and to all my friends; strengthen and comfort the sick and the dying, and those who nurse them: bless all men, and let the whole earth be filled with the knowledge of the glory of the Lord, as the waters cover the sea, through Jesus Christ our Lord. Amen.

II.

EVENING.

Almighty and most merciful Father, let my prayer be set forth in Thy sight as the incense, and let the lifting up of my hands be an evening sacrifice.

Forgive, O Lord, my sins of this day; the sins of my soul and the sins of my body; my presumptuous sins; those which no eye saw but Thine, O Lord; those sins which I have done to please either myself or others. Forgive me those sins which I have knowingly committed, and also forgive my negligences, my want of fellow-feeling with others, my selfishness and self-indulgence, my eagerness or indifference, my irritability and fretfulness, my coldness and want of love.

But, O Lord God, when I have confessed the sins that I know of, they are only a very small part of what Thou knowest of me. Reveal to me those sins which I did ignorantly, and forgive *all* my sin; pardon mine iniquity, for it is great; let the blood of Jesus Christ cleanse me from ALL sin.

O Lord, I praise and bless Thee for all Thy wonderful mercies to me this day, for Thy care over me, Thy love to me, for all the gifts that Thou hast given me, for all the comforts which I have enjoyed, for the strength which Thou hast given me to bear pain, for Thine own presence in loveliness, and for all other mercies so far above all that I could ask or think. Give me a thankful, humble heart, that I may prize each blessing.

Thou hast held me and kept me this day, and now, O Father, into Thy hands I commend my spirit. If Thou hast appointed a wearisome night for me, teach me to be contented with it. If Thou wilt give unto me the blessing of sleep, help me to be thankful; let me not be afraid for any terror by night, defend me under

Thy wings, let me feel that I am safe under Thy feathers, and that Thy faithfulness and truth are my shield and buckler. If I lie awake, keep me, O Lord, from sinful thoughts, drive far from me the enemy, and grant me peace with Thee; thus I shall be kept from the wiles of the devil.

Do Thou fill my mind with holy and heavenly desires, so that there shall be no room for evil thoughts. Let my heart be occupied with Thy statutes, keep me from restlessness, or from saying, Would God it were morning! Grant that I may not be scared with night visions, nor let Thy terrors make me afraid. And, O Lord, if this night I should sleep the sleep of death, let not death have dominion over me. Let me hear Thy voice saying Fear not, for I am with thee, I have redeemed thee. In sleep and in death, O Lord, may I be Thine.

Help me to bear patiently whatever pain and weakness and suffering Thou hast appointed for me. O God of love, teach me to say, Thy will be done.

O Holy Ghost, be with me, and make intercession for me, according to the will of God.

O Saviour of the world, help me to remember Thy Cross and Passion and Thy night of agony.

Bless all the sick and dying, and grant unto them the peace of God and all other blessings this night and evermore. Amen.

III.

MIDNIGHT.

O Lord God Almighty, the earth is keeping silence before Thee now, darkness covers the earth, but the darkness hideth not from Thee, the darkness and the light are both alike to Thee. My Father, look upon me, for Thou neither slumberest nor sleepest. Thou holdest mine eyes waking, I am so feeble that I cannot sleep. Let me feel that I am not alone, that Thou art with me, let Thy rod and Thy staff comfort me. Lord, fill me with Thy fulness, so that all evil thoughts may be kept out. Let not vain thoughts lodge within me. Let not the darkness be a messenger of Satan to buffet me. Speak to my soul, and say unto me, I am Thy salvation. Let not my heart be troubled, and let it not be afraid. Lord, Thou knowest all things; Thou knowest how often the thoughts of yesterday trouble me, and the blackness of the night seems to have settled upon them. I am troubled above measure, yet help Thou me. I have said words that I wish unsaid, but I cannot alter them now. O Lord, prevent them from harming others. I am tempted to magnify words that were said to me; Lord, Thou knowest all, whatsoever it is, that hath so sorely troubled me. Be pleased to deliver me from these snares of the devil: do not let me think unkindly of any who have grieved me. Keep me from dwelling on anything that is past, or any circumstances connected with it. If any have made me sorrowful, help me to pray for them, and grant, O Lord, that whensoever I am made sorrowful, I may be sorrowful after a godly sort.

Purify all my thoughts, cleanse Thou me from secret faults, let the Blood of Jesus Christ Thy Son cleanse me from all sin. Defend me from all the temptations of this night, hide me under the shadows of Thy wings. Let my meditation of Thee be sweet. Lift up the light of Thy countenance upon me, and that shall put joy and gladness into my heart. Then shall the night be light unto me, if Thou, O Lord God, givest me light.

Help me to rest in Thy love; and give unto me that peace which the world cannot give, that whether sleeping or waking I may be with Thee. Help me to lie still and not to grow weary. Give me songs in the night. O blessed Jesus, when Thou wast on earth Thou hadst not where to lay Thy head. Make me very thankful for all the comforts and blessings which Thou hast given me;

and though I cannot spend my sleepless nights in prayer, yet Thou wilt accept the desires of my heart, and wilt make intercession for me.

Be gracious unto all the sick and dying, and in the midst of their suffering, let them feel that Thou lovest them.

Holy Trinity, abide with me this night and evermore. All this I ask through Jesus Christ our Lord. Amen.

IV.

FOR REPENTANCE.

O Lord God, who hast said that Thou hast no pleasure in the death of him that dieth, Thou who hast promised to all them who truly repent and turn to Thee with full purpose of heart, that though their sins be as scarlet, they shall be made white as snow; though they be red like crimson, they shall be as wool, have mercy upon me, pardon and deliver me from all my sins.

O Lord, I believe that though I have sinned, yet I have an advocate with the Father, Jesus Christ the righteous, and He is the propitiation for my sins. For He was wounded for my transgressions, and smitten for my wickedness, and He is the merciful receiver of all true penitents.

O Lord, give me true repentance, help me to submit myself unto Thee, and from henceforth to walk in Thy ways. Help me to follow Jesus in all patience, lowliness, and charity, and to take His easy yoke upon me, so that I may be delivered from the curse of the law.

From henceforth may I be ordered by the government of Thy Holy Spirit. O Lord, vouchsafe to bring me to Thy glorious kingdom, for Thine infinite mercy, and for the sake of Jesus Christ our Lord. Amen.

V.

SORROW FOR SIN.

O Lord God Almighty, Thou art come out of Thy place to visit my wickedness, and how shall I abide the day of Thy coming? I have said, Peace, and all things are safe; I have despised Thy goodness, patience, and long-suffering, which were continually calling me to repentance. Lord, I have abused Thy goodness, which has so often called me to amendment. Yet have mercy upon me, O Lord, after Thy great goodness, according to the multitude of Thy mercies do away mine offences, for I am sorry for my sin. I do earnestly repent, and am heartily sorry for these my misdoings, the remembrance of them is grievous unto me, the burden of them is intolerable; have mercy upon me, most merciful Father; for thy Son, our Lord Jesus Christ's sake, forgive me all that is past, and grant that I may ever hereafter serve and please Thee, in newness of life, to the honor and glory of Thy name, through Jesus Christ our Lord. Amen.

VI.

FORGIVENESS OF SIN.

Jesus, my Saviour, Thou who wert in all points tempted like as I am, yet without sin: have mercy upon me: heal my soul, for I have sinned against Thee. I have offended against Thy holy laws. I have left undone those things which I ought to have done, and done those things which I ought not to have done, and there is no health in me. Jesus, Son of David, have mercy upon me. Lord, lay not this sin to my charge. Wash me thoroughly from my wickedness, and cleanse me from my sins. For I acknowledge my faults, and my sin is ever before me. Turn Thy face from my sins, and put out all my misdeeds. Make me a clean heart, and renew a right spirit within me. For in me dwelleth no good thing. I have sinned against heaven and in Thy sight. Yet speak the word, and Thy servant shall be healed: for Thou hast said, I will heal thy backslidings and love thee freely. Let not sin have dominion over me, that being justified by Thy blood I may be saved from wrath through Thee, and may joy in God, because Thou, O Lord Jesus Christ, hast made atonement for us, so that there is no more condemnation since Thou hast died and art risen again, and art ever at the right hand of God to make intercession for us, and Thine is the kingdom, and the power, and the glory, for ever and ever. Amen.

VII.

FOR FAITH IN THE LORD JESUS CHRIST.

O Lord, my Heavenly Father, without faith it is impossible to please Thee. Have mercy on me, for my faith is very weak.

I believe that Jesus is the Son of God, I love His holy name, and trust Him as my Saviour and my Redeemer, but, O Lord, it is so coldly and so feebly. I am wearied with everything that hinders me, and with the evil and sin of my own heart. Lord, I believe, help Thou my unbelief. O teach me that His name was called Jesus, for He shall save His people from their sins, and that He is exalted to give repentance. Give me repentance, O Lord Jesus Christ, for I am poor and needy. Thou hast promised to give it, without money and without price.

Give me faith, O Jesus, to believe that Thou hast redeemed me, purchased me with Thy precious blood, that I am Thine; and that no man shall pluck me out of Thy hand. Let me believe more simply that Thy blood cleanseth from all sin, and when I sin, O Holy Ghost, convince me of my sin, and make me to know and feel that there is none other name, but only the name of the Lord Jesus, whereby I can obtain health and salvation. Enable me always to look unto Jesus, and to give thanks that we have an advocate with the Father.

I would ask in faith, nothing wavering, but my faith is so weak, that it is like a wave of the sea, driven and tossed. Lord, increase my faith.

Wilt Thou graciously strengthen and confirm it, that I may have daily before me the dying of the Lord Jesus, and may gladly die with Him, and believe that I am risen with Christ, and seek those things which are above, where Christ sitteth at Thy right hand. Help me to be faithful unto death, and never again to doubt Thy promises or Thy love, but to believe that all Thy commandments are right.

Give the same blessing, O Lord, to all who ask it, especially to those who are sick. May we all seek for true faith in Thee, for the sake of Jesus Christ our Lord. Amen.

VIII.

FOR PATIENCE.

O God of patience, make me to be like-minded with Thee. I wish to be patient toward all men; but when I would do good, evil is present with me; the good that I would, I do not; but the evil that I would not, that I do. O wretched man that I am, who shall deliver me from the body of this death? I have thought more highly of myself than I ought to have done, and lest I should be exalted above measure, Thou hast given me this thorn in the flesh, the messenger of Satan to buffet me. I have besought Thee that it might depart from me, for, O Lord, it sorely tempts me to impatience. I cry, Lord, how long, for I fear lest the woe should come on me, because I have lost patience. In weariness and painfulness, in watchings, in hunger, and thirst, O my God, I am tempted to impatience;

Lord, help mine unbelief, for Thou hast said, He that believeth shall not make haste, and that patience must have her perfect work. O give me the patience of Christ Jesus; help me to consider Him, so that I may run the race that is set before me with patience; help me always to be looking unto Jesus, and thus may I bring forth fruit with patience unto all long-suffering with joyfulness.

O my Father, enable me to possess my soul in patience, that I may not grieve the Holy Spirit. I have need of patience; do Thou strengthen me with all might, according to Thy glorious power, for I fall into manifold temptations. Let patience have its perfect work, and do not spare for the crying of the child; only do Thou uphold me in the fiery furnace, so that I shall not be burned, nor the flame kindle upon me. And what I ask for myself, I ask also for all who are tempted in like manner. Let us hear Thy voice saying, My grace is sufficient for thee, My strength is made perfect in weakness. Most gladly then will we rather glory in our infirmities, that the power of Christ may rest upon us, and in our flesh we shall praise God the Father, the Son, and the Holy Ghost. Amen.

IX.

FOR CONTENTMENT.

Jesus, my Saviour, I would follow in the blessed steps of Thy most holy life: help Thou me. Thou didst say, Lo! I come to do Thy will, O God, I am content to do it: O help me to say so. I dare not say it, lest I should draw nigh with my lips, whilst my heart is far off. I love to do Thy will when it pleases me, but I am not contented when my will is crossed. Lamb of God that takest away the sins of the world, forgive me for all my discontented thoughts, and words, and actions. I have not been contented to wait Thy time, I have sought to see the way beforehand. I have not been contented to walk in darkness and have no light, I have not stayed myself upon Thee. I have asked for light, and have thought I did well to be angry because it was Thy will that my way should be hid. O Lord, I cannot have peace until I can rest in Thy love, without asking to see the way by which Thou art leading me. Help me to be contented with all Thy will concerning me: keep me from repining against loneliness: from too great eagerness for human sympathy: from impatience in sorrow; in darkness; under injustice, or the misunderstandings and hard speeches of others. O Lord Jesus, help me to remember that Thou hast borne all these sorrows for me, and that if I learn of Thee who art meek and lowly of heart, all these things will be blessings to me and will liken me unto Thee. Make me to love Thy will in all things, because it is Thy will. Keep me from looking forward even for a day or an hour. Teach me in whatsoever state I am, therewith to be content, to know how to be abased and how to abound. May I receive each trial and each blessing as Thy gift; may I do Thy holy will in all things, and be content with such things as I have, for Thou wilt never leave nor forsake me. May I take no thought for the morrow, and be careful for nothing, but in everything by prayer and supplication make my requests known unto God.

Make me content to live or to die: to suffer or to do Thy will: to be alone, to be sick; to be misunderstood or unknown, just as seemeth good in Thy sight. God the Father help me to rest in Thy love.

God the Son help me to love Thy will.

God the Holy Ghost strengthen and comfort me. Amen.

X.

FOR CALMNESS OF MIND.*

Thou, O Lord Jesus, wast meek and lowly in heart; give me a meek and contrite spirit, as becometh a sinner, yet one who hath hope in Thee. Let me not be unduly cast down or puffed up, let not my soul sink into the depths of despair, let not the waterflood overflow me, neither let the deep swallow me up; let not my heart be haughty, nor mine eyes lofty, lest the steps of my strength be straightened, and my own counsel shall cast me down; lest my confidence shall be rooted out of my tabernacle, and it shall bring me to the king of terrors.

Give me grace, O Lord, to possess my soul in patience; to behave and quiet myself as a child that is weaned of his mother. Let not the extremity of anguish call forth words of bitterness or discontent, or lead me to speak unadvisedly with my lips; but in all my suffering be Thou my support. Let the remembrance of Thy most bitter Passion fill my heart with gratitude, and dispose my spirit to quietness and resignation. Keep thy servant also from presumptuous sins; let them not have dominion over me. The sacrifices of God are a broken spirit, a broken and a contrite heart, O God, Thou wilt not despise.

Give me, O Lord, the fruit of the Spirit, love, joy, peace, long-suffering, gentleness, goodness, faith, meekness, temperance. Let all bitterness, and wrath, and anger, and clamor, and evil-speaking, be put away from me with all malice, that nothing be done through strife, or vain-glory, but in lowliness of mind I may esteem others better than myself. Give me grace, O Lord, to be humble-minded and sober; not soon shaken in mind or troubled, but walking circumspectly; redeeming the time, putting on the breastplate of faith and love, and for an helmet the hope of salvation, in and by Thee, who didst die for us, that whether we wake or sleep, we should live together with Thee. And may the God of Peace sanctify me wholly, and preserve my whole soul, and spirit, and body, blameless unto Thy coming; who livest and reignest with the Father and the Holy Ghost, one God, world without end. Amen.

XI.

FOR HUMILITY.

Out of the deep have I called unto Thee, O Lord; Lord, hear my voice. If Thou, Lord, wilt be extreme to mark what is done amiss, O Lord, who may abide it? But there is mercy with Thee, therefore shalt Thou be feared. Lord, I am high-minded, I have proud looks, I exercise myself in great matters which are too high for me; but Thou hast humbled me and laid me in the dust. Lord, Thou knowest all my desire, and my groaning is not hid from Thee. O do

Thou refrain my soul and keep it low, like as a child that is weaned from its mother; make my soul even as a weaned child.

I have said, God, I thank Thee that I am not as other men are; I have magnified myself, therefore Thou hast brought me low, even to the dust. I have considered the days of old, and the years that are past. O God, childhood and youth alike are vanity; my heart has been lifted up, and I have spoken great swelling words. Help me now, though I have offended, not to offend any more. That which I see not, teach Thou me. Turn Thou me, and I shall be turned; for Thou art the Lord my God. Surely after that I was turned, I repented; and after that I was instructed, I was ashamed; yea, even confounded, because I did bear the reproach of my youth.

O blessed Jesus! teach Thou me; may I learn of Thee to be meek and lowly in heart, that I may find rest unto my soul.

As Thou didst come to visit us in

great humility, so in the last day, when Thou shalt come again in Thy glorious majesty to judge both the quick and the dead, may we rise to the life immortal, through Him that liveth and reigneth with Thee and the Holy Ghost, now and ever. Amen.

XII.

FOR REST IN GOD IN WEAKNESS.

O Father of mercies, and God of all comfort! I flee unto Thee for refuge, until this calamity be overpast. Thou hast brought me very low in a low place. I am so feeble that I cannot speak. Speak, Lord, for Thy servant heareth. I lift up my soul unto Thee. Hear the voice of my humble desire, the voice of my breathing. Help me to be still, and know that Thou art God. I would rest in Thy love. Help me to abide under the shadow of Thy wing, to dwell in Thy secret place. O Lord, my Father, Thou art my refuge and my fortress, my God, in Thee will I trust. Thou hast set Thine house of defence very high, that I may run into it and be safe. My Father, Thy child is very weak and cannot walk alone: Thou hast promised to carry me in Thine arms. I do not ask Thee to renew the strength of this body of sin and death. I do not seek great things for myself: I only ask for strength to trust Thee, and to be silent in Thee; to lie still in Thine arms, and let Thee carry me whithersoever Thou willest; and that Thou wilt give me sure trust and confidence in Thee.

Help me, O Lord, to have no will but Thine, and in everything to be able to say, Even so, Father, for so it seemeth good in Thy sight: and though I have a desire to depart and to be with Christ, yet help me to wait all the days of my appointed time till my change come, and in that hour when Thou wilt say unto me, Come up hither, O righteous Father, be with me: then do Thou answer for me, O Lord my God. O blessed Jesus, who hast tasted death for every man, be with me, and let me feel that I am not alone. O Holy Ghost, the Comforter, be present with me in that hour. O holy Trinity, help me, and all who cry to Thee for succor, to glorify Thee now in sickness, and at the hour of death, and then to praise Thee for ever. Amen.

XIII.

IN PAIN.

Almighty God and merciful Father, to whom belong the issues of life and death, look down from heaven, I humbly beseech Thee, with the eyes of Thy mercy. Of whom can I seek for succor, but of Thee, O Lord, who for my sins art justly displeased?

O Lord, I am chastened with pain upon my bed, and the multitude of my bones with strong pain: so that my life abhorreth bread, and my soul dainty meat. My flesh is consumed away that it cannot be seen, and my bones that were not seen stick out; my soul draweth near unto the grave. I am troubled, I am bowed down greatly, for my loins are filled with a loathsome disease, and there is no soundness in my flesh. Be not far from me, for trouble is near. Our fathers trusted in Thee, and Thou didst deliver them. Hungry and thirsty their souls fainted in them: then they cried unto Thee in their trouble, and Thou didst deliver them out of their distresses.

Thou didst bring them out of darkness and the shadow of death, and break their bonds in sunder. Their souls abhorred all manner of meat, and they drew near unto the gates of death. O Lord, speak the word, and Thy servant shall be healed; or if this be not Thy holy will, yet say unto my soul, I am thy salvation, I will strengthen thee, yea, I will uphold thee with my righteousness; when thou passest through the waters, I will be with thee, and through the floods, they shall not overflow thee; when thou walkest through the fire thou shalt not be burned, neither shall the flame kindle upon thee.

Lord, increase my faith. Look graciously upon all who are in pain; help us all to believe steadfastly in Him who died and rose again, Thy Son our Lord Jesus Christ. Amen.

XIV.

IN INFIRMITIES WHICH HUMILIATE.*

O Lord, rebuke me not in Thy wrath, neither chasten me in Thy hot displeasure; for Thine arrows stick fast in me, and Thy hand presseth me sore. When Thou with rebukes dost correct man for iniquity, Thou makest his beauty to consume away like a moth. Surely every man is vanity. But, O Lord, Thou art with me still, although my soul is cast down, and my flesh wasteth, and I am laid low in the dust; still may I hope in

Thee, and yet praise Thee, the health of my countenance and my God. Have mercy upon me, O God, wash me throughly from mine iniquity, and cleanse me from my sin. Purge me with hyssop, and I shall be clean: wash me, and I shall be whiter than snow. Thou who wast despised and rejected of men, a man of sorrows, and acquainted with grief, have mercy upon me; Thou hast borne our griefs and carried our sorrows; Thou wast wounded for our transgressions, and bruised for our iniquities.

Thou hast sanctified suffering and sorrow, pain and sickness. Lord, give me grace to bring forth their proper fruits. It is good for me that I am afflicted; my spirit was proud, and I needed humiliation; but, O Lord, let me not be utterly cast down; in the depth of my sorrow and my shame be Thou my Comforter; Thou who endurest the Cross, despising the shame, be with me; help me, O Lord, to bear meekly this thorn in my flesh. In great mercy hast Thou given it, lest I should be exalted above measure; let Thy grace be sufficient for me, make my strength perfect in weakness. Lord, I am poor and needy, and my heart is wounded within me, I am like a shadow that declineth; I am helpless and dependent, powerless as an infant, my hands hang down, and my knees are feeble, and my infirmities press hard upon me, and humble me in the sight of man.

But, O Lord, though this chastening for the present seemeth grievous, let it yield to me the peaceable fruits of righteousness. Thou dost chasten me for my profit; let me be partaker of Thy holiness; let that mind be in me which was also in Christ Jesus, who humbled Himself and became obedient unto death, even the death of the Cross. Let me not be wearied and faint in my mind, but endure hardness as a good soldier of Jesus Christ. In His name I come unto Thee for succor; Lord God of mercy, hear my prayer, be with me now and evermore. Amen.

XV.

FOR THOSE SUFFERING FROM HUNGER.

O most merciful God and Father, have pity upon me. I know that as many as Thou dost love, Thou dost rebuke and chasten: and that like as a father pitieth his children, so Thou dost pity them that fear Thee. Thy hand hath touched me. I thank Thee, O Lord, that it has touched me, for by this I know that I am not forgotten by Thee. I do not ask Thee to give me one less pain. I have not shrunk from Thy judgments, for Thou teachest me. O how sweet are Thy words to my taste! I do not ask Thee to change my trials, because Thou hast chosen them for me; and therefore they are sure to humble me and prove me, and show me what is in my heart; and to do me good in my latter end. Yet I have need of Thy grace to help in this time of need. O my Father put strength into me! It hath pleased Thee that I should suffer hunger. My strength is hunger-bitten. I can eat no pleasant bread. O Lord Jesus Christ, Thou wast in all points tempted like as I am, even in this; and Thou art touched with a feeling of my infirmities. For our sakes Thou didst fast forty days in the wilderness alone, with none to comfort Thee. Thou knowest all the great and sore temptations of hunger; for when Thou wert an hungered, the devil came and tempted Thee. O my Saviour, he found nothing in Thee that would yield to him; but he comes to me and finds very much. Thou knowest what the temptations are, and needest not that any man should tell Thee; have mercy upon me, for I am weak. By Thy fasting and temptation, good Lord, deliver me. Keep me from yielding to any temptation, however hidden; and if I sin, speak the words for me, Lay not this sin to his charge. Set a watch on the door of my lips, O Lord, that I may not sin with my tongue. Give me to eat of the hidden manna; and keep before my mind the city which hath foundations, where I shall hunger no more, where there will be bread enough without any scarceness, and I shall eat and be satisfied for ever. Give me patience now under my sufferings, and then, when it pleases Thee, a happy issue out of them all.

Father, Son, and Holy Ghost, hear my prayer which I make unto Thee; I ask these blessings not for myself alone, but for all who are suffering in like manner, and also for the Poor. Amen.

XVI.

FOR THOSE SUFFERING FROM THIRST.

O Lord my God, I would be still, and patient, and gentle, and meek. Thou knowest all things, Thou knowest that I love Thee. As the very hairs of my head are all numbered, so this sore distress which I now suffer is known unto

Thee, and sent by Thee. O Lord, I am one of the poor and needy who seek for water, and there is none, and their tongue faileth for thirst; for my throat is dry, and my heart faileth me, and my tongue cleaveth to my jaws, and my moisture is turned into the drought of summer. O my Father, have mercy upon me. I do not ask that Thou wouldest take away this thirst from me, I only ask Thee to teach me how to make a right use of it. Grant that it may liken me to Thy blessed Son Jesus Christ, for He in His great humility bore this sorrow also; even on the Cross He said, I thirst. O Lord Jesus, since Thou didst thirst, Thou knowest all the pains, and the great and sore temptations, which this trial brings to me. Speak to my heart, and tell me that Thou wilt help me to bear it patiently, and silently, and without murmuring, or showing the impatience which it often makes me feel. May I never try to bear it alone, but always look up to Thee for help: and feel sure that I shall not ask in vain. Help me always to remember that Thou hast redeemed this suffering also, and hast made it a holy thing. Thou didst taste all its bitterness; for Thou wouldest not drink, that Thou mightest suffer with, and for, all who thirst.

O my Father, not my will, but Thine be done; only do Thou fulfil Thy gracious promise, that when the poor and needy seek for water, and their tongue faileth for thirst, Thou the Lord wilt hear them, and wilt not forsake them.

I thank Thee, O Father, that Thou hast said, that after this painful life is ended we shall thirst no more; even now, whilst I am here, O Holy Spirit, enable me, who am athirst, to come and take of the water of life freely.

I ask these blessings, not for myself alone, but for all who are suffering in like manner, through Jesus Christ our Lord. Amen.

XVII.

FOR THOSE IN POVERTY.

O Lord, look down from heaven, behold, visit, and relieve me Thy servant, if it be Thy holy will; but if this is not Thy will, then I beseech Thee to make my will one with Thy will, and not to let me strive against Thee. Thou hast heard me bemoaning myself thus, Surely Thou hast chastised me, and I was chastened; but, O Lord, I have been as a bullock unaccustomed to the yoke. I thank Thee that Thou dost chasten me still, and hast not yet said, Why should ye be stricken any more? ye will revolt more and more.

Lord, Thou knowest all things; Thou knowest that it is not this sickness of my body, this pain and weakness, that tries me the most sharply; if I had that alone, it seems to me it would be easy to bear it. But I cannot work now; I can do nothing, and yet I must live. And for these things my heart is pained within me. Yet, O my Father, I am sure that Thou wouldest not have laid this trial upon me, if it had not been quite necessary for me; for I know that Thou lovest me. Show me wherefore Thou contendest with me. Show me, I pray Thee, the love and the kindness that is in this trial. Teach me how to depend entirely on Thee, O Lord. May I look up to Thee, as my Father who art in heaven, and say, with true child-like trust, Give me this day my daily bread; and if it is Thy will that I should receive that daily bread at the hands of some of Thy children on earth, O Lord, let me be very thankful to them, and give thanks to Thee for putting it into their hearts to minister to me. May I pray for them with thankful love, and have no proud looks, or ever be unwilling to receive Thy gifts through their hands. Ah, Lord God, I know how often I have, in the pride and naughtiness of my heart, tried to find out some reason why Thy servants ought to be kind to me, instead of receiving all their love and kindness as Thy gift.

Grant me, O Lord, more love and more simple trust in Thee; enable me to feel sure that Thou wilt not withhold any good thing from me, only the things that would hurt my soul. Forgive me that I have ever murmured, and help me, O Lord Jesus my Saviour, to remember that Thou hast made poverty a holy state; for though Thou wast rich, yet, for our sakes, Thou didst become poor. I thank Thee that I have a place where to lay my head; though Thou hadst none.

O Lord, forgive me for having ever complained of what Jesus bore so willingly for me; help me ever to remember that for our sakes He made Himself of no reputation, and took on Him the form of a servant, and humbled Himself, that we might suffer *with* Him, so that we can never be alone in our sufferings.

I know O Lord, that Thy judgments are right, and that Thou hast humbled me, and suffered me to hunger, that Thou mightest feed me with manna which I knew not of; make me to learn that man doth not live by bread alone, but by every word which proceedeth out of the mouth of God. Help me now and evermore to say, the Lord is my Shepherd, therefore can I lack nothing; and to believe that goodness and mercy will follow me all the days of my life, and that I shall dwell in Thy house for ever. Grant these blessings, O Father, not to myself alone, but to all who are tried and tempted by poverty, for I ask them in the Name of Jesus Christ; to whom, with the Holy Spirit, be all glory. Amen.

XVIII.

FOR THOSE IN LONELINESS.

O Lord Jesus Christ, Thou who hadst not where to lay Thy head, who for my sake didst tread the wine-press alone; help me to believe that I am not alone, for Thou and the Father art with me. I know that Thou dost allure me and bring me into the wilderness to speak comfortably to me. Thou hast never been a wilderness to me. The wilderness and the solitary place rejoice, and the desert blossoms as the rose, when I feel that Thou art with me, that Thy rod and Thy staff comfort me. O Lord, Thou knowest it is the day of temptation in the wilderness, and sometimes I do not like to sit alone and keep silence, I mourn in my prayer and am troubled, and cry unto the God that setteth the solitary in families, saying, My brother is dead, and I am left alone, Why am I thus? I watch and am alone, as a sparrow on the housetops. I wander in the wilderness in a solitary way, and find no city to dwell in; yet Thou hast dealt well with Thy servant according to Thy word, for Thou dost turn the wilderness into a standing water. Thou plantest fountains in the midst of the valleys, and turnest the hard rock into a springing well.

I bless Thy holy name, for all the way which Thou hast led me in the wilderness, to humble me, and prove me, and show me what was in my heart. Thou art leading me by a right way to the city of habitation. Thou hast fed me in the wilderness with manna, that Thou mightest humble me, and prove me, and do me good at my latter end. Thy way, O God, is holy. Let Thy hand lead me, and Thy right hand guide me: do with me as seemeth good in Thy sight; and when I depart hence, may I come up out of the wilderness leaning on my Beloved, and join the multitude which no man can number, who have come out of great tribulation, and washed their robes, and made them white in the blood of the Lamb. I commend also unto Thee all who are lonely. Help them, O Jesus, to feel that Thou art ever with them, and therefore they cannot be alone. Amen.

XIX.

IN CONFIRMED LONG ILLNESS.*

Look down from Thy throne on high, O Lord, relieve and comfort Thy servant, who crieth unto Thee for patience and endurance in long affliction. It is of Thy mercies that I am not consumed, because Thy compassions fail not, they are new every morning; therefore will I hope in Thee. Thou art good unto them that wait for Thee. Enable me to hope and quietly wait for Thy salvation; I have borne this yoke in my youth, and it hath not passed away. But Thou wilt not cast off for ever, Thou wilt have compassion according to the multitude of Thy mercies, for Thou dost not afflict willingly, nor grieve the children of men. I called upon Thy name, O Lord, out of the low dungeon Thou hast heard my voice; hide not Thine ear at my breathing, at my cry. Grant, Lord, that I may learn obedience by the things which I have suffered.

O Lord, let me labor to enter into that rest which remaineth for Thy people, and if my patience should fall away, renew my repentance: strengthen me upon my bed of languishing, and make all my bed in my sickness. I know not the term of my suffering—months of vanity and wearisome nights may be appointed me. I may grow old in this affliction, and this suffering may find no end save in the grave. It may be that for years my flesh upon me shall have pain, and my soul within me shall mourn; but be Thou with me, Lord, strengthen me with Thy Holy Spirit to the last. Make me glad according to the days Thou hast afflicted me, and the years wherein I have seen evil. All the days of my appointed time will I wait till my change come. I will trust in Thee, and through the mercy of the Most High, I shall not be moved. Hear me, O Lord, in the day of trouble. Send me help from the Sanctuary, and strengthen me out of Zion. Lead me in Thy truth, and teach me, for Thou art the God of my salvation; on Thee do I wait all the day long. Remember, O Lord, Thy tender mercies, and Thy loving-kindnesses, for they have been ever of old. Look upon mine affliction and my pain, and forgive all my sins. O keep my soul and deliver me; let me not be ashamed, for I put my trust in Thee.

Withhold not Thou Thy tender mercies from me, O Lord, let Thy loving-kindness and Thy truth continually preserve me. I am poor and needy, but Thou, O Lord, thinkest upon me. Thou art my help and my deliverer, make no long tarrying, O my God. For Jesus Christ's sake. Amen.

XX.

IN UNCERTAINTY AS TO THE LENGTH AND TERMINATION OF ILLNESS.*

Heavenly Father, Lord God Almighty, all things are known unto Thee. Not a sparrow falleth to the ground without Thee. The very hairs of my head are all numbered by Thee. Thou knowest the term of my days; my times are in Thy hand. Grant me grace in quietness and in confidence to find my strength; let patience possess my soul; let me resign myself into Thy hands, to live or to die, as Thou shalt see best for me. Suspense troubles my mind, and I would not that it were troubled. My spirit is overwhelmed within me, but Thou knowest my path. Thou art my refuge, in Thee do I trust; cause me to know the way wherein I should walk, for I lift up my soul unto Thee. Let me wait on Thee all the day long: extend peace to me like a river: as one whom his mother comforteth, comfort Thou me in sorrow and in weakness, in trouble and in heaviness. Give Thine angels charge over me, to keep me in all my ways.

I know not, O Lord, whether this sickness leadeth me to a speedy death, a release from my bondage, or to long years of suffering and weakness. Lord, I would not, if I might, determine my lot. Thou knowest what is best for me; so teach me to number my days that I may apply my heart unto wisdom: if they be few and evil, open to me the gate of everlasting life: if they be many and oppressed by trouble—if my pain be perpetual, and my wound incurable, Lord Jesus, be Thou beside me; endue me with patience and long-suffering, that my faith fail not, but may endure to the end, rejoicing in hope, patient in tribulation.

Thou, Lord, art Lord both of the dead and of the living; whether I live or die, let me be Thine. Hide me under the shadow of Thy wings. When I walk in the midst of trouble, do Thou, O Lord, revive me; stretch forth Thy right hand to save me. Perfect, O Lord, that which concerneth me. Thy mercy, O God, endureth for ever, forsake not the works of Thine own hands.

Search me, O Lord, and know my heart; try me, and know my thoughts; and see if there be any evil way in me, and lead me in the way everlasting: for the sake of Thy blessed Son, our Saviour Jesus Christ. Amen.

XXI.

IN THE PROSPECT OF AN INACTIVE LIFE.*

Lord Jesus, I cry unto Thee for help. My soul is troubled, and my flesh knoweth no rest. When I lie down, I say, When shall I arise, and the night be gone? I am full of tossings to and fro until the dawning of the day. What is my strength that I should hope? and what is mine end that I should prolong my days? They are past: my purposes are broken off, even my purposes unto good. I sought to serve Thee, O Lord, to do Thy will in activity, but Thou hast chastened me. Thou hast brought this trouble upon me for my good. Teach me to do Thy will in Thine own way, O Lord, in suffering and in patience. Thou willest not that I should work for Thee after the counsel of mine own heart. Thou hast made me of no account; my days are as a shade that passeth away. But, O Lord, I humble myself before Thee: in faithhfulness Thou hast afflicted me, that I might deny myself, and take up my cross, and follow Thee. Lord, I beseech Thee, enable me to present myself a living sacrifice, holy and acceptable unto Thee. Renew my mind, that I may prove what is that good, and acceptable, and perfect will of God, that I may render to Thee a reasonable service.

Lord, I am foolish and weak, but Thou hast chosen the foolish things of the world to confound the wise, and the weak things of the world to confound the things that are mighty; that no flesh should glory in Thy presence. What am I that I should say, I will do this or that good work? Work in me, Lord, for good. I commit my way unto Thee. I trust in Thee, and Thou wilt bring it to pass. In Thy strength alone will I go forth. Teach me to glory only in mine infirmities; casting down imaginations, and every high thing that exalteth itself against the knowledge of God, and bringing into captivity every thought to the obedience of Christ, strengthened with all might according to His glorious power, unto all patience and long-suffering with joyfulness.

Make me perfect, O Lord, in every good work to do Thy will. Work in me that which is well-pleasing in Thy sight, through Jesus Christ, to whom be glory for ever and ever. Amen.

XXII.

FOR HELP IN DELIRIUM.*

Father of mercies, and God of all comfort, I come unto Thee for help and guidance in a time of need. My strength faileth me, my mind is wandering: it is like a wave of the sea driven by the wind and tossed; and I know not the words that may come from my lips, the outpourings of mine anguish; but be Thou nigh at hand, O Lord. Keep Thou the door of my lips, that they may utter no evil thing: let no profane or vain babblings sully them; but in all my extremity may I glorify Thee. Put holy and blessed thoughts into my soul, and help Thou my infirmities. Let the Spirit of Him who raised up Jesus from the dead dwell in me and quicken my mortal body, and lead me to speak that which is right and holy, and pure and good. Let the word of faith be nigh me, even in my mouth and in my heart. Keep my tongue from evil, and my lips from speaking guile. Let my tongue mutter no perverseness: let me bless the Lord at all times: let His praise be continually in my mouth. Instruct me and teach me in the way that I should go. Impute not iniquity to me. Forsake me not, O Lord. O my God, be not far from me. Make haste to help me, O Lord, my salvation. I am feeble and sore broken, I am ready to halt. I can take no more heed to my ways, but be Thou with me, Thou art my Father; I am the clay, Thou art the Potter. Take heed for me that I sin not with my tongue; keep my mouth with a bridle.

Withhold not Thou Thy tender mercies from me, O Lord: let Thy lovingkindness and Thy truth continually preserve me. In the night that darkens my soul, let Thy song be with me, and my prayer be unto the God of my life: let me not be cast down and disquieted within me: let me still hope in Thee and praise Thee, the health of my countenance and my God. Restore unto me the joy of Thy salvation, and uphold me with Thy free Spirit. Redeem my soul from the power of the grave. What time I am afraid, let me trust in Thee.

Save and deliver me, O Lord God, Father, Son, and Holy Spirit, be with me, now and ever. Amen.

XXIII.

FOR HELP IN RESTLESSNESS.

In Thee, O Lord, have I put my trust; let me never be put to confusion, but rid me and deliver me in Thy righteousness.

I have trusted in Thee, O Lord; I have rested in Thee, and in Thee my soul rests now. My soul is silent before Thee, O Lord; but my spirit is grieved because of this restlessness, and that I am so often tossing to and fro, and seeming to those about me as if my heart were disquieted within me. Lord, Thou knowest all things, Thou knowest that my spirit is at rest, though the flesh is weak. But man looketh on the outward appearance, and cannot tell how much I desire that even the quietness of my body should show forth Thy praise.

I would lie still, but I cannot do this of myself; Thou canst enable me to do it; Thou canst keep me from saying, in the morning, Would God it were evening! and in the evening, Would God it were morning! Thou canst keep me from that restlessness which distresses me, and which makes me wish so often to change my posture, and to change my place, if it were possible. I cannot resist this alone; I have not strength even to hide from others the pain that I feel. Be Thou my stronghold, whereunto I may alway resort; Thou hast promised to help me, for Thou art my house of defence and my castle. Go not far from me, O God! My God, haste Thee to help me. O help me to abide patiently, and to praise Thee ever more and more. Thou art my only help in time of need;

help me to fly unto Thee for succor, whenever this restlessness comes on. The more the outward man decayeth, so much the more, O Lord, I shall need that Thou wouldst strengthen me continually with Thy grace and Holy Spirit in the inner man. To him that hath no might, Thou hast promised to increase strength. O my Father, when the last hour draws near, I pray Thee in great mercy then help me to lie still, and to feel the everlasting arms underneath me, supporting, and strengthening, and comforting me. If I speak, grant that they may be peaceful and holy words; if I am silent, may I rest wholly in Thee, and then I shall not be confounded. Hear my prayer, also, O Lord, for all who suffer in this way, and grant to them the blessings which I have asked for myself, in the name and for the sake of Jesus Christ our Lord. Amen.

XXIV.

IN THE PROSPECT OF AN OPERATION.*

Jesus, my Redeemer, my Saviour, Thou who didst not despise the Cross, but didst yield Thyself to the tormentors, who didst drink of the cup of sorrow willingly, yet didst taste of its bitterness, be Thou with me in the hour of my agony; strengthen me to bear all that shall be laid upon me: in every pang may my spirit still have power to say with Thee, Not my will, but Thine be done.

For the thing which I greatly feared is come upon me, and that which I was afraid of is come unto me. But I will cast my burden upon Thee; O Lord, do Thou sustain me. From the end of the earth will I cry unto Thee, when my heart is overwhelmed: lead me to the rock that is higher than I. Give me grace, O Lord, to yield up my will into Thy hands, to trust in Thee, in Thy might, and in Thy providence, rather than in the skill of man. Do Thou bless it, Lord, if so it seemeth good in Thy sight, for my relief; but if not, if it should be in vain, let me still bless and praise Thee, and submit myself to Thy good pleasure. Let me go to this trial in the strength of the Lord God, committing myself to Him that judgeth righteously. Lord, it may be that this remedy shall fail; then, let patience have its perfect work in me. It may be that it shall open to me the gates of life, that this light affliction, which is but for a moment, may work for me a far more exceeding and eternal weight of glory. Even so, Father, if so it seemeth good in Thy sight.

Only, whether I live or die, let me be Thine, O Lord, and know Christ and the power of His resurrection, and the fellowship of His sufferings, being made conformable unto His death, who shall change our vile body, that it may be fashioned like unto His glorious body, according to the working whereby He is able even to subdue all things unto Himself. Into Thy hands I commend myself, O Lord God of my salvation. Amen.

XXV.

IN GREAT WEAKNESS.

O Lord, Thou hast said that to him that hath no might, Thou dost increase strength. I have no strength: have mercy upon me, O Lord, for I am weak. I am brought low, even unto the dust of death. I am poured out like water. Attend unto my cry, for I am brought very low.

I know that I must pass through this weakness. I do not ask Thee, O Lord, to renew the strength of my body. I am content to do Thy will, to be low in a low place. Yet, O Holy Father, let it be Thy pleasure to deliver my soul. O Lord Jesus Christ, it was when Thou wast an hungered, that the devil came and tempted Thee; he tempts me now in my

PRAYERS FOR THE SICK.

weakness to doubt Thy love, and to think that a strange thing has happened to me.

By Thine hours of weakness, blessed Jesus, deliver me.
By Thy faintness and exhaustion,
By Thine aching frame,
By Thy failing strength,
By Thy wearied spirit,
Blessed Jesus, deliver me.
When fainting by the way—in sickness and sorrow,
Most merciful Jesus, deliver me;
From murmuring thoughts,
From forgetfulness of Thy love,
From speaking hastily, or in anger,
From pride and self-will,
From self-indulgence and self-pleasing,
From impatience under crosses,
Blessed Jesus, save and deliver me.

Speak unto my soul and say, The battle is not yours, but God's. O Lord God, fight for me and help me to hold my peace.

I know, O my Father, that my strength is to be still; but I want to feel Thy strength. Help me to believe that the Eternal God is my refuge, and that underneath me are the everlasting arms, that Thou wilt thrust out the enemy before me, saying, Destroy them.

Help me to rest in Thy love. Thou knowest that I love Thee, but let me show forth my love to Thee; let others take knowledge that I have been with Jesus, that He is with me now, even in this dark valley; let them see that the Holy Ghost, the Comforter, is with me.

Grant this, O Father, not to me alone, but to all who are weak, for Jesus Christ's sake. Amen.

XXVI.

IN GREAT WEAKNESS AND INABILITY TO PRAY.

O Lord, to whom all hearts be open, and from whom no desires are hid, hear the voice of my desire. I look up unto

Thee, my heart panteth, my flesh faileth, my thoughts are as water spilt upon the ground which cannot be gathered up. I am poured out like water. O Lord, forsake me not when my strength faileth. I am as a man that hath no strength. My heart is smitten, and withered like grass, my bones cleave to my skin. O Lord, my spirit waxeth faint, for Thou hast added grief to my sorrow: I fainted in my sighing, and I find no rest. Thou hast sent a faintness into my heart, so that the sound of a shaken leaf chases me: I have no power to stand before my enemies. I have fainted, and wished in myself to die, and said, It is better for me to die than live. Yet when my soul fainted in me, I remembered the Lord, and my prayer came in unto Thee, into Thine holy temple. Let the voice of my breathing come unto Thee.

O Lord, Thou hast said that when the poor and needy seek water, and there is none, and their tongue faileth for thirst, Thou wilt hear them, and Thou, the God of Israel, will not forsake them. I would not faint now that I am rebuked of Thee; but I cannot lift up the hands which hang down, and the feeble knees. Increase strength to me, O my Father, for I have no might. The earthly house of my tabernacle is being dissolved. Grant that I may faint not: though the outward man perish, let the inward man be renewed day by day. Out of weakness may I be made strong. Though I am very weak, yet, O Lord Jesus, may I be weak in Thee, and with Thee, who, though Thou wast crucified through weakness, yet now livest by the power of God.

Grant, O Lord, that whilst I lie here on this bed, and cannot think one thought of my own, or say any words of prayer, I may be found in Thee, not having mine own righteousness.

O Jesus, pray for me, for I am Thine. Be Thou glorified in me. Keep me from evil. Sanctify me through Thy truth. Do Thou answer for me, O Lord my God. O Holy Spirit, make intercession for me with groanings which cannot be uttered, and help me to feel that it is good for me that I am afflicted and brought so very low, that I may cease from my own works and be crucified with Christ. Grant these blessings, O Lord, to me and to all who are suffering with me in this trial of great weakness. In the hour of death, and in the day of judgment, good Lord, deliver us, for the sake of Jesus Christ our Lord. Amen.

XXVII.

IN GREAT SICKNESS.

O Lord, I know that the way of man is not in himself, it is not in man that walketh to direct his steps. Thou hast hedged in my way. The thing which I greatly feared is come upon me, and that which I was afraid of is come unto me.

I was not in safety, neither had I rest, neither was I quiet, yet trouble came. It is come upon me, and I faint; it toucheth me, and I am troubled. The things that my soul refused to touch are as my sorrowful meat. Even to-day is my complaint bitter, my stroke is heavier than my groaning. Show me wherefore Thou contendest with me. Wilt Thou contend against me with Thy great power? No; Thou wilt put strength into me. Thou knowest the way that I take; and when Thou hast tried me I shall come forth as gold. Thou art in one mind, and who can turn Thee? and what Thy soul desireth, even that Thou doest. For Thou performest the thing that is appointed for me.

I know, O Lord, that Thy judgments are right, and that Thou, of very faithfulness, hast afflicted me. Let, I pray Thee, Thy word be for my comfort, for no chastening for the present seemeth to be joyous, but grievous; O make it afterward to yield the peaceable fruits of righteousness to me who am exercised thereby. Do Thou strengthen my weak hands, and confirm my feeble knees. Say to me, who am of a fearful heart, Be strong, fear not. Come and save me, O Lord: help me to believe that these light afflictions are but for a moment, and that they will work out for me a far more exceeding and eternal weight of glory. May I look not at the things which are seen, but at the things which are unseen; for the things which are seen are temporal, but the things which are unseen are eternal.

Grant this, O Lord, to me and to all who are sick, for the sake of Jesus Christ, our Mediator and Advocate. Amen.

XXVIII.

IN SORE TROUBLE.

O Lord Jesus Christ, when Thou wast in an agony Thou didst pray the more earnestly, help me now to pray. I am in an agony, O Lord, but I cannot pray, for my spirit waxeth faint, and my soul is sore troubled, the enemy cometh on so fast. I am feeble and sore broken. When I cry and shout, Thou shuttest out my prayer; it cannot pass, for mine iniquities are gone over my head, and are too heavy for me to bear. Mine enemies live and are mighty; they say unto my soul, There is no help for thee in God. O Lord, how long? Let it be Thy pleasure to deliver my soul. When I cry unto Thee, then shall my enemies be turned back. But, O Lord, they daily return, and they be many that fight against me, O Thou most High.

Save me, O God, for the waters are come in unto my soul. I stick fast in deep mire where there is no standing. I am come into deep waters where the floods overflow me. I am weary of my crying, my throat is dried, mine eyes fail while I wait for my God. O God, Thou knowest my foolishness, and my sins are not hid from Thee. Deliver me out of the mire, and let me not sink; let me be delivered from them that hate me, and out of the deep waters. Hear me, O Lord, for Thy loving-kindness is good; turn to me according to the multitude of Thy tender mercies, and hide not Thy face from Thy servant, for I am in trouble. Hear me speedily, I am poor and sorrowful. For Thou hearest prayer, Thou despisest not the prisoners. I will yet praise Thee, and will magnify Thee with thanksgiving; and will say with my whole heart, Glory be to the Father, and to the Son: and to the Holy Ghost; as it was in the beginning, is now, and ever shall be: world without end. Amen.

XXIX.

FOR THOSE WHO ARE VERY ILL.

O Saviour of sinners, who camest to seek and to save that which was lost, have mercy upon me. Thine arrows stick fast in me, and Thy hand presseth me sore. In the cutting off of my days,

I shall go to the gates of the grave, I am deprived of the residue of my years. I shall behold man no more, with the inhabitants of the world. Thou wilt cut me off with pining sickness; but let it be Thy pleasure to deliver my soul. O let my soul live, and it shall praise Thee: in Thy favor is light: in Thy light let me see light. I know, O Lord, that Thy judgments are right, and that Thou of very faithfulness hast caused me to be troubled. I have not shrunk from Thy judgments, for Thou teachest me. That which I see not, teach Thou me. It is good for me that I have been afflicted, that I might learn Thy statutes. But, O Lord, I am oppressed, undertake for me. They be many that fight against me, O Thou most High. Nevertheless, though I am sometimes afraid, yet put I my trust in Thee. Thou art my Helper and Redeemer. O Lord, make no long tarrying; enable me, and all who are very ill, to embrace and ever to hold fast the blessed hope of everlasting life which Thou hast given us in our Saviour Jesus Christ. Amen.

XXX.

FOR THOSE WHO HAVE GIVEN WAY TO IRRITABILITY.

Jesus, my Saviour, my Redeemer, I have sinned against heaven and in Thy sight, I have spoken unadvisedly with my lips, and sinned with my tongue; I have been angry without a cause, and have grieved Thy Holy Spirit. I said in my haste, words that I ought not to have said; I did not cease from anger, or forsake wrath. Against Thee have I sinned, O Lord, for Thou hast said, Let all bitterness, and wrath, and anger, and clamor, and evil-speaking be put away, and be ye kind one to another. I have provoked one of Thy servants to anger, and thus I have sinned against my own soul. Holy Father, I dare not plead before Thee that I did not mean the words that I said; for if I had set Thee, the Lord, continually before me, I should not have spoken these words; if I had set a watch before my mouth, and kept the door of my lips, I should never have spoken these hasty words. I dare not plead with Thee, O Lord, that my pain made me speak so hastily; for Thou didst send the pain, and I know that Thou canst send the strength to bear it. O Lord, I declare my iniquity, I am sorry for my sin; and Thou hast said, that if we confess our sins, Thou art faithful and just to forgive us our sins, and to cleanse us from all unrighteousness. Have mercy upon me, O Lord, after Thy great goodness, and according to Thy loving-kindness do away mine offences. O blessed Jesus, by Thy Cross and Passion, by Thy precious death and burial, by Thy glorious resurrection and ascension, and by the coming of the Holy Ghost, have mercy upon me. Give Thy heavenly blessing to her whose heart I have discouraged, and whose spirit is sore vexed.

Let her not, O Lord God of Hosts, be ashamed for my cause. Let not those that seek Thee be confounded through me, O Lord God of Israel; and from henceforth may I show forth Thy power with all patience and long-suffering. Speak unto me, O Lord, and let me hear Thy voice saying, Thy sins are forgiven thee: go, and sin no more. Vouchsafe, O Lord, to keep me this day without sin, for Jesus Christ's sake. Amen.

XXXI.

FOR THOSE WHO WALK IN DARKNESS.

O Lord my God, help me to feel that Thy hand is leading me, that Thy right hand is guiding me. Thou knowest the way that I take, and when Thou hast tried me I shall come forth as gold. Let me feel that it is Thou Thyself, my Father, who art leading me through this great and terrible wilderness. I can see the pillar of the cloud sometimes going before me; but I walk on in darkness, having no light.

Even now, O Lord, help me to stay myself on Thee, to flee unto Thee, to hide me in the rock, and in the holes of the rock. I do not ask to see light here, if that is not Thy holy will. I ask only that I may submit myself wholly to Thy will and pleasure, and cry, Jesus Son of David, have mercy upon me. Lord, help mine unbelief. I have been searching and trying Thy ways, O Lord, and have forgotten that it is the glory of God to conceal a thing; and therefore Thou hast made my way dark and slippery.

I have sinned, O Lord, I have sinned and done this evil in Thy sight; yet have mercy upon me after Thy great goodness, and do away mine offences. With my whole heart have I sought Thee, O let me not go wrong from Thy commandments. Before I was in trouble I went wrong, but now I desire to keep Thy word.

O Lord, I do not ask for the life of my

body; but let my soul live, and it shall praise Thee. In Thy favor is life, and my life is hid with Christ. Grant that I may indeed know in whom I have believed.

If Thou wilt, O Lord, be pleased to lift up the light of Thy countenance upon me, and grant me peace. But if it is not Thy good pleasure to deliver my soul here, help me to say from my heart, Though Thou dost slay me, yet will I trust in Thee. And when the earthly house of this tabernacle is dissolved, then may my eyes see the King in His beauty, because He has washed me from my sins in His own blood. Amen.

XXXII.

FOR THOSE WHO HAVE FORGOTTEN GOD IN TIME OF HEALTH.

O Lord, I have heard Thy speech, and was afraid, for I have forgotten Thee; how shall I come and appear before Thy presence? Yet in wrath remember mercy. Thou hast chastised me, and I was chastised; but, Lord, I am like a bullock unaccustomed to the yoke. I thought that Thou wast a hard master, reaping where Thou hadst not sown, gathering where Thou hadst not strewed; and I went and hid my talent in the earth.

I thought to remember Thee, and to call upon Thee whenever sickness came, and that I should have time then to make my peace with Thee, and might go on enjoying myself until then. It is come upon me now, and I am shut up, I cannot go forth, and none of those things which I have so delighted in give me any comfort. Desire hath failed; and those who would come to amuse or comfort me, miserable comforters are they all. O Lord, I am afraid; I dare not lift up my eyes, or pray to Thee, for I have forgotten Thee ever since I became a man (woman). I was taught about Thee when I was a child; but I put away those thoughts as childish things, and now I cannot pray. I thought it would be easy whenever illness should come upon me. O Lord, I have destroyed myself: sickness is come, and I am too weak to think, and my mind is taken up with my pains, and I cannot seek Thee as I would. I put it off to a more convenient season, and now what shall I do? where shall I hide myself from Thy presence if I die?

O spare my life, spare me yet a little longer, that I may try to seek Thee. I have heard that Thou art a God willing to pardon iniquity, and that the blood of Jesus Christ cleanseth from all sin.

O pardon my sin, especially the sin of having forgotten Thee for so many years; and teach me now about Thyself, and all that I need to learn; and, O Lord, let me not die until my sins are pardoned, and I have found that there is mercy with Thee. Lord, teach me to pray: O let me live, and I will try to serve Thee better. O that I had remembered Thee, that I might have hope and comfort now.

Sickness presses hard upon me. O Lord, I cannot pray, I cannot understand Thy holy Word, yet, O Lord, have mercy upon me; Christ, have mercy upon me; and do not leave me to perish now that Thou hast shown me that I am a sinner: teach me all that I need to learn, and forgive all my sin, for the sake of Jesus Christ our Lord. Amen.

XXXIII.

FOR THE BACKSLIDER IN HEART.

Righteous art Thou, O Lord, yet let me plead with Thee of Thy judgments. I have hewn out for myself cisterns, broken cisterns, which can hold no water, and have departed from the living God. O Lord, Thy sentence has justly come upon me,—The backslider in heart shall be filled with his own ways; and Thou hast added grief unto my sorrow: I fainted in my sighing, and I find no rest. O that it were with me as in months that are past, when the candle of the Lord shined upon me, and by His light I walked through darkness! O that I knew where I might find Him: I go forward, but He is not there; and backward, but I cannot perceive Him; on the left hand, where He doth work, but I cannot behold Him. Yet I cannot be forgotten before Him; for He hath hedged up my way with thorns, so that I cannot get out. I followed after my idols, but I could not overtake them. I forgot the Lord my Maker until He sent me this pining sickness, and called my sins to remembrance; and now I remember my ways and all my doings wherein I have been defiled; and I loathe myself in my own sight for all the evils that I have committed. I will return unto the Lord, for I have greatly sinned. O Lord, wilt Thou plead against me with Thy great power? Wilt Thou not put strength into me? For there is forgiveness with Thee, that Thou mightest be feared: Thou art plenteous in mercy, O turn Thee, and have mercy upon me; for I am in trouble. Thou dost chasten me in measure; I thank Thee that Thou dost not leave me wholly unpunished, and hast not yet said, Why should ye be stricken any more? ye will revolt more and more.

O God, give me grace to be zealous and repent. I have lived in pleasure, and been dead whilst I lived, and have grieved the Holy Spirit; yet, O Lord, Thou hast not quite left me. Who is a God like unto Thee, that pardoneth iniquity? Pardon mine iniquity, for it is great. I hear Thy voice speaking to me now by this sickness, saying unto me, I will allure thee, and bring thee into the wilderness. I do not ask Thee to speak comfortably to me, but to give me repentance; for I have sinned against Thee, and am no more worthy to be called Thy son. Chasten me, O Lord, as Thou seest best for me; but O suffer me not to depart from Thee again. May I from this time cry unto Thee, My Father, Thou art my guide; and may I follow on to know the Lord, and walk in holiness as long as Thou willest that I should stay here on earth.

Grant this, O Lord, for Jesus Christ's sake. Amen.

XXXIV.

FOR THOSE WHO FEAR THEY MAY HAVE BEEN DECEIVED.

O Lord God, my soul is sore amazed, and I am brought into great trouble. The end of all things seems at hand to me; and I fear lest even at last I should be weighed in the balance and found wanting. O if Thou shouldest cast me off, then I should have no place to flee unto; for whither can I go from Thy presence? If I said to the mountains and to the rocks, Fall upon me, and hide me from the face of Him that sitteth upon the Throne, and from the wrath of the Lamb, I could not flee from Thy presence, for the darkness hideth not from

Thee. I thought I was Thy child, O Lord, and that I loved Thee; but my love is so cold that I sometimes fear that I never have loved Thee at all, and have deceived myself.

O speak to me, and say unto my soul that my sins are forgiven, that Thou hast blotted them out for Thine own name's sake. If I have never come to Thee before, help me to come now at the eleventh hour. Give me true repentance, and let me not deceive myself in any way. Search me, O God, and know my heart; try me and know my thoughts, and see if there be any wicked way in me, and lead me into the way everlasting. Lord, help my unbelief. Give me even now to believe that the blood of Jesus Christ cleanseth from ALL sin. And though I may have but a short time to live, let me feel hope that Thou hast heard my prayer. O, blessed Jesus, who didst hear the prayer of the thief on the cross, hear my prayer. Graciously look on my affliction, and say unto me that my sin is forgiven, and mine iniquity is covered, and that Thou wilt not impute my transgressions to me; and then, Lord Jesus, receive my spirit. Amen.

XXXV.

FOR THOSE WHO ARE SUFFERING FROM WANDERINGS OF MIND IN WEAKNESS.

O God of love, by Thy great and endless pity attend unto my cry, for I am brought very low. Hear the voice of my groaning, for my groaning is not hid from Thee. I try to show before Thee my trouble, but my thoughts run hither and thither unto the ends of the earth. I call upon Thee daily, and in the night season make my prayer unto Thee; and I know that Thou dost not count my words as vain, though they seem so to me. O Lord, the loftiness of man Thou layest low, that Thou alone mayest be exalted in that day; I believe that this is the day of Thy visitation, and that Thou alone wilt be exalted, and I must be abased; I thank Thee, O Lord of heaven and earth, for this chastening. It is thus that Thou wilt reveal Thyself to me, and show me things which were hidden from me, when I thought that I was wise and prudent.

O Lord God, Thou knowest that I would keep my mind always stayed on Thee, and that my heart would always talk with Thee. Have mercy upon me, for I am weak. I put my full trust only in Thy mercy, and abide under the shadow of Thy wings; Thou wouldest have me to do so; in this I cannot err from Thy commandments. O my Father, Thou hast made the keepers of the house to tremble, and the strong man to bow himself. I cannot remember even Thy words; I cannot meditate in Thy statutes, though my delight is in Thy law. Do Thou work all Thy works in me: if Thou dost work, none can hinder it. As for me, I am poor and needy, but the

Lord careth for me. How precious are Thy thoughts unto me, O God! they are more precious unto me than gold, yea, than most fine gold.

O Lord Jesus, Thou didst promise to Thy disciples that the Holy Spirit should bring all things to their remembrance whatsoever Thou hadst spoken to them, I ask only to remember Thy words, not my words, or my prayers, or anything that has been spoken to me, except what Thou willest that I should remember.

Accept my memory, my understanding, my entire will. Whatsoever I have or possess, Thou hast of Thy bounty bestowed upon me. All this I restore unto Thee, and surrender it to be disposed of according to Thy will. Only give me love for Thee along with Thy grace, and I am rich enough; I ask for nothing more. And as I am not alone in this trial, have pity on all who are suffering from it, and bless it to us all. Grant unto us these blessings, O Holy Trinity, and we will alway give thanks unto Thee. Amen.

XXXVI.

FOR THOSE WHO FEEL THE DIFFICULTY OF PRAYER IN WEAKNESS.

Lord, teach me to pray. I know not what I should pray for. Let Thy Spirit help mine infirmities. I am feeble and sore smitten. O my Father, before I was afflicted I went up into Thy temple to pray, and joined with the multitude that kept holy day. But it was often the prayer of the Pharisee which I said there. I thank Thee for having abased and humbled me, and made me to know that I can of my own self do nothing. Lord, teach me to pray; teach me what is the prayer which Thou wilt hear. I come to Thee as a little child to rest in Thy love. God be merciful to me a sinner.

O Lord, in time past I have wearied Thee with words; but now I have no words to bring, my thoughts are as water spilt upon the ground, which cannot be gathered up. Thou hast said, Watch and pray, lest ye enter into temptation. O Jesus, say for me now what in Thy love and pity Thou didst say for Thy disciples: The spirit indeed is willing, but the flesh is weak. My eyes are very heavy; and when I try to watch and pray, Thou comest and findest me asleep. O Lord Jesus, my comfort is, that Thou hast entered within the veil, there to make intercession for me. O Lord, unto whom all hearts be opened, and from whom no desires are hid, cleanse the thoughts of my heart, and hear the voice of my humble desire, the voice of my breathing.

Help me, Lord Jesus, to ask the same blessings for all that are sick and dying; and do Thou pray for us, that we all may be one in Thee, as Thou and the Father art one. Amen.

XXXVII.

FOR THOSE WHO HAVE BEEN TAKEN UP WITH THE CARES OF THIS LIFE, AND BEEN OVER ANXIOUS.

O Lord God, Thou hast laid affliction upon me, Thou hast call me aside. I know it is Thy voice speaking to me, but as yet I cannot say, My ears hast Thou opened; they are dull of hearing. Show me wherefore Thou hast afflicted me. Have I not served Thee, O Lord; I have gone with the multitude to Thy house, I have kept holy day, I gave tithes of all I possessed, I fed the poor, and what lack I yet? O Lord, I hear Thy voice saying to me, thou art rich and increased in goods, yet knowest not that thou art miserable, and poor, and blind. O teach me to buy of Thee gold that I may be rich. I know that when earthly riches increased, I set my heart upon them; but I did not feel till now how sinful it was to do so. The cares of this world sprang up and choked the good seed. I thought I was serving Thee in all this, by doing what was right to my family; but this sickness says to me, Seekest thou great things for thyself? seek them not. O Lord, turn away mine eyes from beholding vanity, and quicken me according to Thy word. My heart is disquieted within me. O God, I wish to be still, but I am careful and troubled about many things. I know that one thing is needful, but my thoughts are busy about the things of this life. I am troubled above measure; teach me how to be careful for nothing, but in everything to give thanks; teach me how to cast all my care upon Thee, for Thou carest for me. Grant that Thy peace may rule in my heart and mind. O teach me how, with prayer and supplication, and thanksgiving, to let my requests be made known unto Thee. And if it be Thy holy will that I should recover my bodily health, may I try to live more simply for Thee, and as in Thy sight;

may my moderation be known unto all men, and may I ever remember that the Lord is at hand.

Forgive my past sins, O Lord, and my forgetfulness of Thee. May I ever give Thee thanks, that Thou didst call me aside, and draw my heart nearer to Thyself. O let me not forget Thee, if I go forth into the world again. Let not these prayers rise up in judgment against me, but spare me, good Lord, and lead me into Thy truth and teach me, from this time forth, and for evermore, for I ask all in the name and for the sake of Jesus Christ our Lord. Amen.

XXXVIII.

FOR THOSE WHO FEEL THE WANT OF SYMPATHY.*

Lord, I am desolate and oppressed, hide me under the shadow of Thy wings. I am alone, bereft of human sympathy, but Thou art with me. Thy rod and

Thy staff they comfort me. Thou knowest my down-sitting and mine uprising; Thou understandest my thought afar off. Thou hast known my reproach, and my shame, and my dishonor. Reproach hath broken my heart; and I am full of heaviness: I looked for some to take pity, but there was none; and for comforters, but I found none. They sought to strengthen me with their mouth, and that the moving of their lips should assuage my grief; but they vex my soul, and break me in pieces with words. They understand not my griefs; the bitterness of my heart is hidden from them. They are physicians of no value, the soreness of my wounds they cannot heal; but Thou, O Lord God, heavenly Father, Thou art my help; leave me not, neither forsake me, O God of my salvation. I had fainted unless I had believed to see the goodness of the Lord in the land of the living. O how great is Thy goodness which Thou hast laid up for them that fear Thee; which Thou hast wrought for them that trust in Thee before the sons of men! Hide me, O Lord, in the secret of Thy presence, from the pride of man, keep me secretly in Thy pavilion from the strife of tongues.

Thou, O Lord Jesus, Saviour of the world, wast despised and rejected of men, oppressed and afflicted, bruised and put to grief; for the Lord laid on Thee the iniquity of us all. Thou wilt not leave me comfortless, Thou wilt come unto me. Who shall separate us from Thy love? shall tribulation, or distress, or persecution, or famine, or nakedness, or peril, or sword?

Let the sense of my loneliness here draw me nigher Thee, O my Saviour; let it not breed any bitterness in mine heart toward my fellow-creatures; but let me be tender-hearted and forgiving, gentle unto all men, apt to teach, patient; remembering mine own infirmities, and committing myself to Him who judgeth righteously. In Thy name and to a loving Father I make my prayer. Amen.

XXXIX.

THAT SUFFERING MAY NOT PRODUCE SELFISHNESS.*

Grant, O Lord God, merciful Father, that this visitation may turn to my salvation, that I may consider my ways, and root out the spirit of evil, the love of self; that in the extremity of anguish, I may not shut my heart against the sufferings of others; that I may not look only on my own things, but on the things of others, remembering that God so loved us that He sent His Son to be the propitiation for our sins, to be wounded for our transgressions, and bruised for our iniquities, and to lay down His life for us; and that if God so loved us, we ought also to love one another. O Lord, let this chastisement enable me more entirely to suffer with them that suffer, to soothe their sorrows, to have compassion on their infirmities, to love them, not in word or in tongue, but in deed and in truth. Lord, I fear lest my heart should grow hardened, and I should shut up my bowels of compassion from my suffering brethren; lest the sense of mine own pangs, and the tender indulgence of those around me, should lead me to think only of myself, to be unmindful of them, to dwell only on my own afflictions, and to think lightly of the far greater trials that others are called to suffer.

Give me, O Lord, that most excellent gift of charity, the bond of perfectness, that I may put on, as the elect of God, bowels of mercies, kindness, humbleness of mind, meekness, long-suffering, bearing others' burdens, seeking by sympathy to soothe and lighten them; as I have opportunity, doing good unto all men, especially unto them that are of the household of faith; not weary in well-doing; that being rooted and grounded in love I may be able to comprehend, with all saints, what is the breadth, and length, and depth, and height, and to know the love of Christ which passeth knowledge; that I may be filled with all the fulness of God. Now unto Him that is able to do exceeding abundantly above all that we ask or think, according to the power that worketh in us, unto Him be glory in the Church, by Christ Jesus, throughout all ages; world without end. Amen.

XL.

FOR THE AGED.

Lord, Thou hast been our dwelling-place in all generations. With long life hast Thou satisfied me, and shown me Thy salvation. I thank Thee, O my Father, for all the blessings of this life, for all the many mercies which Thou hast given me; they are more in number than the sand. Bless the Lord, O my soul, and forget not all His benefits. Thou hast redeemed my life from destruction, and crowned me with mercy and loving-kindness; and I look back on all the way by which Thou hast led me, and see that it was the right way to the city of habitation. I thank Thee for all that Thou hast given me, and for all that Thou hast taken away, and for all the sorrows which have led me to Thee.

Teach me now to number my days, that I may apply my heart unto wisdom. O my Father, I need Thy help now more than I ever needed it before; for though by reason of strength, the days of my years are fourscore years, yet is my strength but labor and sorrow. The years are come in which I say, I have no pleasure in them; the keepers of the house tremble, the strong men bow themselves, the grinders cease because they are few, and those that look out of the windows are darkened. I am often afraid of that which is high, and fears are in the way. O God, Thou knowest those fears, how many they are; not one is unnoticed by Thee; and Thou pitiest me, though I seem to others so weak and foolish. Desire has failed; I cannot tell what I wish for, my thoughts change, and my judgment is very slow.

The grasshopper is a burden; every thing now is a weariness to the flesh. O my Father, Thou knowest how very hard this is for me to bear. Thou knowest how often these things tempt me to be angry and impatient, and to think that other people are unkind to me. Help me to be patient under these sufferings, O Lord; to feel that it is Thy will that I should bear them; and when I am tempted to be hasty, or to think that those about me are slow, and not trying to please me, may I try to be dumb and to keep silence, because it is Thy doing. O keep the door of my mouth, and let no angry, or impatient, or complaining words proceed out of it. And do Thou grant unto me that I may bring forth fruit in my old age, to show that Thou art upright, and that Thou art my Rock.

Help me to remember how many are suffering as I am: may I feel for them, and pray for them; and when it shall please Thee, wilt Thou so fetch us home, blessed Lord, that we may be saved through the merits of Christ Jesus our Saviour. Amen.

XLI.

FOR ONE AFFLICTED WITH BLINDNESS.

O Lord Jesus Christ, when Thou wast upon earth, Thou didst give sight to the blind, and Thou carest for them still; have mercy upon me, Jesus, Thou Son of David. I do not ask Thee to give me back the sight which it was Thy holy will to take from me; but, O Lord, I ask to have patience under this suffering. I ask to be made quite willing to bear it so long as I live. Keep me, I pray Thee, from all fretful thoughts, from all murmuring, from sad thoughts when I am alone and have no outward things to cheer me.

Help me to remember the many mercies which Thou hast given me, and the blessings and comforts which are still granted to me. Thou knowest how much I have loved, when the winter was past, to see the flowers appear, and the face of the earth renewed. O my Father, I shall behold these things no more, with the inhabitants of the earth; and sometimes, because of this, mine eyes weep sore, and I am troubled above measure.

O Almighty God, who alone canst order the unruly wills and affections of sinful men, so order my will that it shall have no variance from Thy will, and that my whole heart may say, Thy will be done.

My heart's desire and prayer to Thee is, that as Thou hast closed my eyes to all earthly things, Thou wouldest open the eyes of my mind, that I may see Thee, O Lord: and as the remembrance of the sight of earthly things fades away, may I see heavenly things more and more clearly; may I endure, as seeing Him who is invisible, and feel that, whereas I was blind, now I see. O merciful God, Thou knowest all the hindrances and temptations which this trial brings, and yet Thou never takest away one blessing, without giving more than Thou takest away. Give me to see Thee, O Lord; draw me nearer to Thee each day, and make me to feel the greatness of Thy love, and this shall comfort me. Have mercy upon all who are blind, and give them the same blessings which I ask for myself, for the sake of Jesus Christ our Lord. Amen.

XLII.

FOR ONE AFFLICTED WITH DEAFNESS.

O blessed Jesus, Thou who didst Thyself take our infirmities, that Thou mightest understand them, and be a merciful and faithful High Priest: Thou knowest my infirmity, for Thou hast sent it to me. Almighty God, have mercy, for this is a very grievous trial to me. I can no more hear the voice of joy and melody; and when I go up to the house of the Lord, I cannot hear the voice of prayer and of thanksgiving, for I am a deaf man, which heareth not. And when my children are gathered around me, I cannot hear their voices, which used to gladden me. It is only when I am alone that I forget my infirmity; Thou knowest, Lord, what temptations and trials it brings to me. O keep me from all unkind, and unloving, and suspicious thoughts of others; keep me from all complaining; deliver me from murmuring thoughts, from causing my trials to be a trial to others; graciously prevent it, O Lord, from making my temper irritable or trying to others. O keep my soul, and deliver me; do not let me sin against Thee, or wish my lot or my trial different to what Thou hast ordained it. And when I am with others, may I be always cheerful, and remember that, though I seem to myself then the most solitary, I am never alone, for Thou art with me, Thy rod and Thy staff they comfort me. Help me to look forward with thanksgiving to the day when the ears of the deaf shall be unstopped, and though with my outward ears I can hear no more, yet, O Lord, I pray Thee to open my heart to Thy truth. And now that I cannot be distracted with outward voices and sounds, may I see the blessing there is in this privation, and make a right use of it, and ever be watching to hear what the Lord will say unto me; and listening for Thy still small voice: may I never lose anything that Thou dost speak to me, but say always, Speak, Lord, for Thy servant heareth.

O hear me and answer me, my Father; not for myself alone do I ask these blessings, but for all who have the same infirmity. O God of patience, give us all patience to the end, for Jesus Christ's sake. Amen.

XLIII.

IN WEARISOME NIGHTS.

O Lord Jesus Christ, Thou knowest that in the night season I take no rest; sleep is gone from me: when I lie down I say, when shall I arise and the night be gone? I am full of tossings to and fro unto the dawning of the day, for Thou scarest me with night visions; I am afraid of the terror by night. Thou hast tasted this suffering for me, for in the night season Thy soul was exceeding sorrowful, even unto death; have pity upon me now; give me grace to feel that wearisome nights are appointed unto me. O my Father, God of love, Thou neither slumberest nor sleepest, the darkness and light are both alike to Thee; the night shineth as the day; Thou art about my path, and my lying down, and art acquainted with all my ways; therefore I will fear no evil, Thy rod and Thy staff comfort me. Thou wilt visit me in the night season; in the night Thy son shall be with me, and my prayer unto the God of my life, so that even the night shall be light about me; by night I have sought Thee on my bed, and Thou hast heard me. O let the fire of Thy love give light in the night, and then I shall not say, would God it were morning, for I shall have songs in the night. Unto Thee, O Lord, will I sing, and will praise Thy name, because it is so comfortable. I know, O Lord, that though weeping may endure for a night, joy cometh in the morning, and there shall be no night there, for the Lord God giveth light, and the days of our mourning shall be ended. Help me now, O Father, Son, and Holy Ghost, to be of good courage; strengthen mine heart to wait patiently on Thee. Amen.

XLIV.

FOR SUNDAY.

Almighty and most merciful Father, who dwellest not in temples made with hands, Who hast said, Unto this man will I look, even to him that is poor and of a contrite spirit, and trembleth at my word.

O Lord Jesus Christ, who art the Head of the body, the Church, the fulness of Him that filleth all in all.

O Holy Ghost, the Comforter, be with me, I pray Thee; I, who am the prisoner of the Lord, pray Thee to let my cry come before Thee, for I am shut up, I cannot go into the house of the Lord. Thou hast shut me up. Thy will be done.

Yet, Lord, I have loved the habitation of Thine house, and the place where Thine honor dwelleth. As the hart panteth after the water-brooks, so longeth my soul after Thee, O God: when shall I come to appear before God? For I had gone with the multitude; I went with them to the house of God, with the voice of joy and praise, with a multitude that kept holy-day.

My soul longeth, yea, even fainteth for

the courts of the Lord: my heart and my flesh crieth out for the living God. For a day in Thy courts is better than a thousand. Blessed are they that dwell in Thy house, they will be still praising Thee. O Lord God of Hosts, hear my prayer; give ear, O God of Jacob. O Lord, Thou hast said unto me, Enter into thy chambers, and shut thy doors about thee. In the way of Thy judgments, O Lord, have I waited for Thee; the desire of my soul is to Thy name, and to the remembrance of Thee. Thou hast brought me to Thy banqueting-house, and Thy banner over me is love. Make me to be planted in Thy house, and to flourish in the courts of our God. I will worship toward Thy holy temple, and praise Thy name, for Thy loving-kindness and for Thy truth. I will praise Thee with my whole heart. Help me in this my prison to sing praises unto the Lord, and to rejoice and be glad because of Thy judgments. Grant the same blessings to all who are the prisoners of the Lord, to those who are sick, and to those who are kept from Thy house in nursing them. Preserve all Thy sick members in the unity of the Church, and may we evermore sing praises unto Thy holy name, O Father, Son, and Holy Ghost. Amen.

XLV.

FOR A BLESSING ON THE USE OF MEDICINE AND OTHER REMEDIES.*

Thou, O Father of Mercies, healest the broken in heart, and bindest up their wounds. Thou givest medicine to heal their sickness, and healest all their diseases. Thou hast created medicines out of the earth. Grant, I beseech Thee, Thy blessing to the means used for my relief, if so it seemeth good unto Thee. Thou, O blessed Jesus, didst not despise the use of human remedies. Thou didst anoint the eyes of the blind to give him sight. Thou canst bless the simple things of the world for my relief, yet without Thy blessing the wisdom of the world is foolishness, the skill of man is as nothing, and his medicines are worthless as the dust of the earth that is blown away by the wind.

Thou makest sore, O Lord; if it seemeth good to Thee, do Thou bind up my wounds. Thou woundest, and Thy hands make whole. Thou canst strengthen the weak hands and confirm the feeble knees. Unto thee do I look for succor: I am feeble and sore smitten, there is no health in my bones; but Thou, O Lord, canst heal mine infirmities, Thou canst recover me, and make me to live. I submit myself to Thee to live or to die as shall seem best in Thy sight. If it please Thee that this remedy, this balm for my pain, should assuage it, and restore my strength, to Thee, O Lord, be the praise: if it please Thee that it prove of none avail—if Thy sentence is, in vain shalt thou use many medicines, for thou shalt not be cured; if the cup of suffering may not pass from me except I drink it, Thy will be done.

Lord, give me strength to suffer, and to will and to do Thy good pleasure. Strengthen me on the bed of languishing, make Thou all my bed in my sickness.

Be with me now and evermore, for the sake of Thy blessed Son, Jesus Christ. Amen.

XLVI.

THAT SICKNESS MAY BRING FORTH ITS PROPER FRUITS.*

Lord God of mercy, great hath been Thy loving-kindness unto me. In great mercy hast Thou afflicted me, to lead me in paths of righteousness, to heal me of my wounds. Grant, Lord, that this suffering may not be in vain. Thou hast turned Thine hand upon me, purely purge away my dross, O Lord, and take away all my tin: purify and purge me as gold and silver in the refiner's fire, that I may offer unto Thee an offering in righteousness: let me be Thine in the day when

Thou makest up Thy jewels. When Thou givest me the bread of adversity, and the water of affliction, let mine ears hear a voice behind me, saying, This is the way, walk ye in it, when ye turn to the right hand and to the left. Teach me Thy way, O Lord, and lead me in a plain path. I am afflicted very much; quicken me, O Lord, according unto Thy Word. I will lift up mine eyes unto the hills, from whence cometh my help. My help cometh from the Lord. Suffer not my foot to be moved from the narrow way that leadeth unto life. Heal me, O Lord, and I shall be healed; save me, and I shall be saved. Thou knowest my foolishness, and my sins are not hid from Thee. That which I see not teach Thou me. Thou makest sore, and bindest up; Thou woundest, and Thine hands make whole. Lift me up, O Lord; I humble myself before Thee. I am bound with fetters, and holden in cords of affliction. Show me my work, and my transgressions that I have exceeded; open my ear to discipline, that I may return from mine iniquity, denying ungodliness and worldly lusts, and living soberly, righteously, and godly in this present world, looking for that blessed hope, and the glorious appearing of the great God and our Saviour Jesus Christ.

Thy judgments are right, in faithfulness hast Thou afflicted me; let, I pray Thee, Thy merciful kindness be for my comfort.

Thou Who art the Captain of my salvation, Who wast made perfect through suffering, sanctify my sufferings to me.

In all my affliction, Thou art afflicted. Let the Angel of Thy presence save me: in Thy love, and in Thy pity, redeem me, O Lord my Saviour. Amen.

XLVII.

TO BE ENABLED TO GIVE THANKS FOR SUFFERING.

O Blessed Jesus, help me to feel that there should be no greater comfort than to be made like unto Thee, by suffering patiently adversities, troubles, and sicknesses. Thou Thyself wentest not up to joy, but first Thou didst suffer pain. Thou didst not enter into Thy glory before Thou wast crucified. Most gladly, therefore, would I glory in my infirmities; but for the present they are not joyous to me, but grievous.

Thou art touched with a feeling of my infirmities; Thou wast in all points tempted as I am; and Thou didst say, Father, save me from this hour; If it be possible, let this cup pass from me. O Thou Man of sorrows, who art acquainted with grief, I thank Thee for those gracious words.

My spirit indeed is willing, but my flesh is weak; and I am afraid of Thy judgments. Yet, O my Saviour, I would by any means attain to the resurrection of the dead. I would suffer with Thee, that I may also reign with Thee.

Help me now to rejoice in my sufferings, and to fill up that which is behind of the afflictions of Christ in my flesh. Make me to walk worthy of the Lord unto all pleasing, and to be fruitful in every good work, and increasing in the knowledge of God. O Lord, I am sick nigh unto death, but do Thou have mercy upon me.

Thou didst humble Thyself, Jesus, my Redeemer, and becamest obedient unto death, even the death of the Cross. I bless Thee, that it is given to me, not only to believe on Thee, but also to suffer for Thy sake. May I be filled with the fruits of righteousness, unto the glory and praise of God, abounding therein with thanksgiving, giving thanks always, for all things. I ask these blessings not for myself alone, but for all who are called to the fellowship of Thy sufferings; and may the Holy Ghost, the Comforter, abide with us, and the peace of God, which passeth all understanding, keep our hearts and minds, through Jesus Christ. Amen.

XLVIII.

THE PURPOSE OF SUFFERING IS TO LIKEN US TO THE SON OF GOD.

O Lord, my heavenly Father, Thou hast sent me this long sickness, and it is not joyous to me but grievous. Keep me from either despising Thy chastising, or fainting when I am rebuked of Thee. Teach me to know that I can never suffer alone, because Christ hath borne my griefs and carried my sorrows; help me to rejoice, inasmuch as I am a partaker of His sufferings. O Lord, from henceforth enable me to count this a very high honor; and may I take up my cross gladly, and follow Him, and rejoice that I am counted worthy to suffer. Help me to rejoice in tribulation, and always to give thanks for this Thy will concerning me.

O Lord, forgive me for looking so much at my pains and sufferings, and so little unto Jesus. Help me to remember His Agony and Bloody Sweat, His Cross and Passion, and this will make my cross easier to bear. O my Father, I have too often wished that there were some easier way to inherit eternal life: but Thou knowest all things, Thou knowest that I love Thee, and that my heart's desire is that I may know the love of Christ, which passeth knowledge, and be filled with all the fulness of God, that I may be found in Christ, not having mine own righteousness, but that which is through the faith of Christ; that I may know Him, and the power of His resurrection, and the fellowship of His sufferings, being made conformable unto His death. O my Father, if Jesus suffered these things before He entered into His glory, how much more ought I to suffer who have so greatly sinned! I thank Thee that He tasted death for every man, and overcame its sharpness, and opened the kingdom of heaven to all believers.

Help me evermore to reckon the sufferings of this present time as not worthy to be compared with the glory which is to be revealed. Enable me, O Lord Jesus, to look upon these light afflictions as but for a moment. For the joy that is set before me, may I endure the cross. O Jesus, the Captain of our salvation, Thou wast made perfect through suffering, perfect the work which concerneth me, by suffering also. Send me whatever Thou seest needful for me; only leave me not, neither forsake me. And help me to learn obedience by the things which I suffer. Grant this to me, O Lord Jesus Christ; and not to me only, but to all who are sick and suffering. O Holy Ghost, Thou dost take of the things of Christ, we beseech Thee to show them to us, and evermore to keep before us His Cross and Passion, His Death of Agony. Amen.

XLIX.

FOR THOSE WHO BELIEVE THAT DEATH IS COMING NEAR AND DESIRE IT, BUT ARE TOLD IT IS FAR DISTANT.

O my Father, hear me, my heart is disquieted within me. I have longed, yea, even fainted, for the courts of the Lord. My heart and my flesh cry out for the living God. I thought that the day of rest was near, that it had almost come, I was glad and gave thanks to Thee. I had requested for myself that I might die, and said, it is enough, now, O Lord, take away my life. My soul had fainted, and I had wished in myself to die, and said, it is better for me to die than live. Search me, O God, and know my heart, try me, and know my thoughts, and see what way of wickedness is in me, and lead me in the way everlasting.

O my Father, I have been deceiving myself, and thereby I have deceived others. Thou alone knowest how much of self-will there has been in this desire. Thou knowest how often weariness of this long sickness, or being grieved and wearied with my sins, and finding the burden of them intolerable, has made me desire to depart. Sometimes the way has seemed so very long, and as if it had no end, and my soul was discouraged because of the way, and then I grew impatient. Thou knowest all the secret causes far better than I know them myself; for my faults are not hid from Thee. O my Father, I know that I have been asking to be at rest more than that Thy holy will might be done in me in any way that Thou pleasest. I have not quietly left it to Thee to choose for me when I should depart.

I thank Thee now with my whole heart that Thou hast kept me here until Thou hadst taught me that in all this I have sinned, and been unlike unto my

Lord and Master, Jesus Christ, who came from heaven, not to do His own will, but the will of the Father who sent Him. If I had been like Him, O Lord, I should have waited patiently; I should not have been striving with Thee as I have done, or wished for rest one moment before Thou dost send it. I have thought that what was *my* will was Thy will, I made an idol of it and worshipped it. But Thou wouldest not leave me; Thou hast taught me, and had patience with me; and Thou hast shown me that my hour is not yet come, and made me willing to abide in the flesh, and continue here, because it is Thy will. O my Father, it seemed very hard to me when first I was told that I should live for many years and suffer all that time. I thought that he who said it was as one that mocked; but Thou didst send him to humble me, and prove me, and show me what was in my heart. I thought they were only the words of a man, but he was Thy messenger, O Lord; and if

I had heard Thy voice speaking, I should not have rebelled or murmured.

Thou hast shown my sin to me; it has found me out. But O! it is a very difficult lesson to learn. My Father, Thou hast taught me hitherto, do not leave me now, but bend my will to Thy will, and make my whole heart to say, Thy will be done. O my Father, if it be possible, let this cup pass from me; yet teach me to say, not as I will, but as Thou wilt. I have besought Thee to let me depart, but Thou hast said, my grace is sufficient for thee. O make me content with this gracious answer. O my God and Father, keep me from thinking so much of the words of a man that must die. My times are in Thy hands, not in his. Thou hast appointed unto me a set time, and wilt remember me.

Thou hast ordered who shall go first, and each one that shall follow, every man in his own order. O grant that I may never be impatient again; all the days of my appointed time enable me to wait willingly, cheerfully, patiently, enjoying life, and seeing good days, because it is Thy holy will, O God of Love; and may I ever feel sure that, when the right hour comes, the prayer shall be answered, Father, I will that they also whom Thou hast given me be with me where I am, that they may behold my glory. O God the Father, God the Son, and God the Holy Ghost, hear, and answer, and pity, and strengthen me; and what I ask for myself, I ask for all to whom the same trial is appointed. Be with me, and with all my fellow-sufferers, and give us patience to the end. Amen.

L.

FOR THOSE WHO ARE RECOVERING FROM SICKNESS, AND HAVE THE PROSPECT OF RETURNING TO ACTIVE LIFE.

O Lord, I will give thanks to Thee, for Thou art good, and Thy mercy endureth for ever. The sorrows of death compassed me, I found trouble and sorrow, and by my sickness was brought nigh unto death.

But Thou, O Lord, hadst mercy on me; and not on me only, but also on my family. Thanks be to Thee, O Lord, for Thy marvellous loving-kindness: for Thou didst bring me to the gates of death, and yet Thou didst turn again and refresh me, and comfort me on every side.

What shall I render to the Lord for all His benefits to me? I will take the cup of salvation, and call upon the name of the Lord. I will pay my vows unto the Lord, now in the presence of all His people, in the courts of the Lord's house. The Lord hath chastened me sore, but He hath not given me over to death. I shall not die but live, and declare the works of the Lord. Thou art my God, and I will praise Thee. Thou art my God, and I will exalt Thee. Thou hast dealt bountifully with Thy servant, O Lord; Thou hast brought me health and cure, be pleased also to reveal to me the abundance of peace and of truth.

O Lord, Thou hast in great mercy renewed my strength, grant, I beseech Thee, that since this sickness is not unto death, it may be fo Thy glory, that the Son of God may be glorified hereby. Thou hast chastened me for my profit, that I might be a partaker of Thy holiness; now that I am going forth again to do my duty in that state of life unto which Thou hast called me, if I do not serve Thee more purely and entirely, surely this sickness will rise up in judgment against me.

O Lord, in my sickness I said, I will take heed unto my ways, that I sin not with my tongue. I said I would serve Thee all the days of my life, that I would love Thee with all my heart, and all my mind, and all my strength, if I might but recover my bodily health. O let not any prayers that I have offered rise up to condemn me. Let me not break any of the vows which I made when I thought I should die, but help me, O Almighty God, daily to perform those vows, and from henceforth to do justly, and love mercy, and walk humbly with Thee, as I have never done before.

O Lord, it is not in man that walketh to direct his steps. I cannot keep these vows, I have no might. Give, therefore, Thy servant an understanding heart. Teach me Thy way, O Lord, and I will walk in Thy paths. Lead me in Thy truth, and teach me, for Thou art the God of my salvation.

Grant, O most merciful Father, I beseech Thee, that through Thy help I may both faithfully live and walk according to Thy will in this life present, and also may be partaker of everlasting glory in the life to come. Grant the same help and blessings, O Lord, to all who are now recovering from sickness, for we ask it in the name of Jesus Christ our Lord. Amen.

LI.

PRAYER BEFORE RECEIVING THE SACRAMENT OF THE LORD'S SUPPER.

Almighty Father, who hast given Thine only Son to die for our sins, and to rise again for our justification; grant me so to put away the leaven of malice and wickedness, that I may alway serve Thee in pureness of living and truth. Help me now to keep this feast, not with the old leaven, but with the unleavened bread of sincerity and truth. I will arise and go to my Father, and say unto Him, Father, I have sinned against heaven and in Thy sight, and am no more worthy to be called Thy child. I am not worthy that Thou shouldest come under my roof; and yet Thou sayest, Behold, I stand at the door and knock: if any man hear my voice I will come in to him, and sup with him, and he with me.

O my Father, I beseech Thee to open

the door of my heart: if Thou dost open, no man can shut it. I have often been so lovingly called by Thee, O Lord; and yet how often I have refused to come!

Lord Jesus, I have dared to disobey Thy last commandment, and have lived as if Thou hadst not said, Do this in remembrance of me. I have heard the words, Come unto me, all that travail and are heavy laden, and I will refresh you. But I did not come to Thy Holy Table, when I had health and strength, and might have come: dare I venture now, O Lord, when I am so weak and ill? must I not stay away now? I am afraid I could not give my attention, I am so weak, and my mind wanders: and yet, O my Father, Thy poor weak child never needed the living Bread which came down from heaven so much as now, which if a man eat thereof, he shall not die. My strength and my heart faileth; this bread will strengthen my heart. Thou didst call to the marriage feast the lame, the halt, and the blind. O

Lord, do not let Satan persuade me that my sin is too great to be forgiven; for Christ Jesus came into the world to save sinners; and if any man sin we have an Advocate with the Father, Jesus Christ the righteous.

O Lord Jesus Christ, Thou hast said, With desire have I desired to eat this passover with you, before I suffer. O let not the desire be all on Thy part, and the unwillingness on mine. If Thou desirest that I should come to Thy table, Jesus, my Saviour, take away all unbelief, and unwillingness, and slowness of heart, and want of love, and purify my soul, even as Thou art pure. Let me see God, which only the pure in heart can do: may I simply believe Thine own words, and take, and eat: because it is Thy Body, and Thy Blood. For Thy flesh is meat indeed, and Thy Blood is drink indeed: whoso eateth Thy flesh hath eternal life. Help me to believe Thy words, for they are past my understanding; and from henceforth may I thankfully and with a glad heart come to Thy holy Table, until it pleases Thee to grant that I may drink new wine in the kingdom of my Father, with the great multitude which no man can number. O Holy and Blessed Trinity, grant these mercies now and evermore. Amen.

LII.

FOR THE CHURCH AND THE CLERGY.

Almighty and everlasting God, we pray Thee to hear the prayers of the sick members of Thy body the Church, for all estates and conditions of men. Let Thy continual pity cleanse and defend Thy Church; and because it cannot continue in safety without Thy succor, preserve it evermore by Thy help and goodness. Give us grace seriously to lay to heart the great dangers we are in by our unhappy divisions; take away all hatred, and prejudice, and whatever else may hinder us from godly union and concord, that as there is but one body, and one spirit, and one hope of our calling, one Lord, one faith, one baptism, one God and Father of us all, so we may henceforth be all of one heart, and one soul, united in one holy bond of truth and peace, of faith and charity, and may with one mind and one mouth glorify Thee. Most merciful Father, we beseech Thee to hear us in behalf of all bishops, priests, and deacons, not only those who are laboring in this country, but also in all other countries, in the colonies, and in heathen lands. Send down, O Lord, upon all Thy servants Thy heavenly blessing, that they may be clothed with righteousness, and that Thy word spoken by their mouths may never be spoken in vain. May it please Thee to give to all Thy people increase of grace to hear meekly Thy word, and to receive it with pure affection, and to bring forth the fruits of the Spirit, and truly to serve Thee in holiness and righteousness of life.

I pray for all the clergy who are related or known to me, especially those for whom my prayers are desired. And, O Lord, hear my prayer particularly for him who ministers to me in holy things, and whom Thou hast appointed to watch for my soul as one that must give account. Grant that I may ever cause him to give that account with joy, not with grief. May I learn humbly, meekly, and thankfully whatever he teaches me. May I never be a hindrance to him, or to his work, or any stumbling-block to others; and because I cannot go up to the house of the Lord, may I receive his ministrations the more thankfully, and try to practise what he teaches me. Give Thy heavenly grace to him, O Lord, and daily increase in him Thy manifold gifts of grace, the spirit of wisdom and understanding, the spirit of counsel and ghostly strength, the spirit of knowledge and true godliness, and fill him with the spirit of Thy holy fear, now and for ever. Grant these, and all other blessings which we have failed to ask, in the name, and for the sake of Jesus Christ our Lord. Amen.

LIII.

FOR THE FRIENDS WHO ARE WITH US, AND THOSE WHO ARE ABSENT, AND FOR NURSES AND ATTENDANTS.

O Lord, Thou hast been, and Thou art gracious unto Thy servant. Thou hast never suffered me to lack any good thing. Is the disciple above his Master, O Lord? My Saviour in His agony and Passion was forsaken even by His own disciples; but I have never been left alone in my lighter suffering. Thou hast in great mercy always sent me kind friends to care for and serve me; and Thou hast put such love and patience into their hearts, that they have borne patiently with my long sickness, with all the trouble I have given them, and with my waywardness and irritability. I confess before Thee, O my Father, that sometimes I have been difficult to please, and perverse, and wilful, and have grieved them by words and deeds; I have not been considerate of them as I ought to have been, and have been unthankful. I have too often received their service as a right, instead of as a good gift, and a work of charity in them; and yet Thou hast given to them such love and forbearance that they still have patience. Bless, Lord, with holy blessings, all who have ever nursed me, or ministered to me in any way; those who are with me now, and those who of necessity are absent. Bless especially [my parents], and remember for good all their unwearied love, and patience, and tenderness, which Thou didst give them, and which they have so richly measured out to me. Bless [my brothers] and [sisters], and let them have full measure, pressed down, returned to them sevenfold in all the gifts of the Holy Spirit. Bless also, O Lord, with Thy fatherly blessing, the dear friends whom Thou hast so wonderfully raised up for my needs, to comfort and to tend me; may they have the blessing of the Lord, which maketh rich, and addeth no sorrow thereto. Bless all who have ministered to me in holy things, who have taught, or admonished, or comforted me, or who have given me to eat and to drink of Thy Body and Thy Blood; let not this labor of love be forgotten before Thee.

Bless the medical men who have attended me, and may they ever look upon themselves as Thy ministering servants, sent forth to minister to Thy children. Bless the servants of the family who have been so faithful and kind to me, and especially bless her who has so long served me with unwearied and faithful love. May she be rewarded an hundredfold. I commend her to Thy fatherly love and care; increase in her true religion, nourish her with all goodness, and of Thy great mercy keep her in the same.

Bless also all strangers who have ministered to me. I cannot recompense them, or any that have been kind to me; but Thou wilt recompense them at the resurrection of the just.

O Lord, Thou hast brought me to great dependence on those who nurse me; I thank Thee that Thou hast also made me willing to be dependent, that Thou hast taken from me the slavish dislike to giving them the trouble that is necessary; for it was pride that made me wish to be independent, and do everything for myself.

O God, forgive my sins to all who have been about me, or ministered to me; and give them day by day to feel, when they minister to the sick, that they minister to Christ Himself, who has said, Inasmuch as ye did it unto one of the least of these, ye did it unto Me. Let them find that even a cup of cold water given to a disciple in the name of a disciple shall in no wise lose its reward. Bless those of my dear family and friends who now lie sick upon their beds; comfort them, O Lord, and comfort all who are sick; and when these light afflictions are ended, may we meet in Thy holy presence, to go no more out. These blessings we ask for Jesus Christ's sake. Amen.

LIV.

FOR MEDICAL MEN.*

O Lord Jesus Christ, Who art the Great Physician of our souls, shower down Thy blessings, I beseech Thee, on those who devote themselves to the sick in body, (and especially on . . . . . .) Look Thou favorably on their labors, bless the means which they use to the relief of suffering, and the strengthening of weakness. Without Thee, O Lord, vain is the help of man. May they go forth to their work in the strength of the Lord God, not trusting in their own wisdom, but looking to Thee for guidance, and acknowledging that to Thee belong the issues of life, and the issues from death, and that of the Most High cometh healing; praying to Thee the prayer of faith that shall save the sick, working not for their own profit or their own glory, but for the good of man and the glory of God. Let the consideration of His works, the operations of His hands, how fearfully and wonderfully we are made, how curiously wrought, lead their minds to the praise and worship of the Creator, in whose book all our members were written, when as yet there were none of them. In all their ways may they acknowledge Thee, direct Thou their path, O Lord. Add to their faith, virtue, knowledge, temperance, patience, godliness, brotherly kindness, charity. Give them, O Lord, the spirit of love and of gentleness, teach them how to soothe the sick and comfort the weak-hearted, to strengthen the diseased, to heal that which is sick, to bind up that which is broken, to bind up their wounds tenderly, and to heal them with healing medicines and with balm. Bless them, O Lord, in all their labors. Be Thou to them a shield and a buckler, preserve them from the terror by night, from the arrow that flieth by day, from the pestilence that walketh in darkness, and from the destruction that wasteth at noon-day, when a thousand fall at their side, and ten thousand at their right hand, let it not come nigh them: let no evil befall them, let no plague come nigh their dwelling.

Reward them, O Lord, for all their loving-kindness to Thy smitten children. Accept it as done to Thyself, forget not their work and labor of love; and when Thou comest in Thy glory, and all the holy angels with Thee, let them be accounted good and faithful servants, and may they hear Thy voice, saying, Inasmuch as ye have done it unto the least of these my brethren, ye have done it unto Me. Let them enter into Thy joy, and live with Thee, Who livest and reignest with the Father, and the Holy Spirit, One God, blessed for evermore. Amen.

LV.

THANKSGIVING FOR FRIENDS.*

Blessed be Thy Name, O Lord my God. Great have been Thy mercies to me, and the blessings by which Thou hast lightened the trial of suffering to which Thou hast called me. Lord, Thou hast not left me destitute or comfortless. Thou hast raised up friends to soothe mine affliction, and to comfort me in my sorrow. Thou hast crowned me with loving-kindness and tender mercies. Though sickness has shut me out from many, yet it has drawn others to whom I looked not for comfort nearer to me. Thou hast not put my brethren far from me, neither are mine acquaintances estranged from me: my kinsfolk have not failed me, nor have my familiar friends forgotten me. They whom I loved are not turned against me: their tenderness still comforts me, their love is very pleasant to me. And for these and all Thy mercies I desire to praise Thee, O Lord, Heavenly Father, Author of all mercies, from Whom cometh every good gift.

Thou, O Lord Jesus, hast sanctified human affection: there were those on earth whom Thou didst esteem dear unto Thee, and didst honor with Thine especial love. I thank Thee that this blessing is not denied me, that I have friends who love at all times, and brothers born for adversity.

As in water face answereth to face, so doth the heart of man to man. Give me grace, O Lord, to profit by this blessing; let me never turn their hearts from me by coldness, or by a contentious spirit. May their love for me work good and not evil to them. May we be bound together in the bonds of Christian affection. May our prayers for each other ascend to Thee. Reward Thou them fourfold for their good offices to me; and grant that we may all hereafter live and reign with Thee, Who livest and reignest with the Father and the Holy Ghost, one God, blessed for evermore. Amen.

LVI.

THANKSGIVING FOR BODILY COMFORTS.*

Thy tender mercies, O Lord, are over all Thy works. The eyes of all wait upon Thee, and Thou givest them their meat in due season. Thou openest Thine hand, and satisfiest the desire of every living thing. I will praise Thee, O Lord my God, I will give Thee thanks for all Thy mercies. Thou hast given me the good things of this world abundantly, to lighten the burden of my sickness. Thou dost comfort me when I lie sick upon my bed, and makest my bed in all my sickness. Thou hast blessed the tenderness and the skill of man to provide me with comforts whereby the sick are soothed and eased in the extremity of their suffering and of their weakness. Blessed be Thy name, O Lord, for all these alleviations of my sickness. Thy blessed Son, our Lord Jesus Christ, though He was rich, yet for our sakes became poor, that we, through His poverty, might be rich. Many are called to endure both poverty and sickness, who lodge without clothing, and have no covering in the cold; who are wet with the showers of the mountains, and embrace the rock for want of a shelter. What am I, Lord, that Thou hast made my lot to differ? But I have all, I abound, I am full; I am enriched in every thing to all bountifulness. May I never forget from whose hands all my comforts come. What have

I that I did not receive from the living God, who giveth us richly all things to enjoy? May they fill my heart with thankfulness to Thee, and with compassion to those from whom they are withheld. And shouldest Thou see fit at any time to take them from me, grant me, O Lord, in whatever state I am therewith to be content, to know both how to be abased and to abound; both to be full and to be hungry, both to abound and to suffer need. I look unto Thee, O Heavenly Father, for my daily bread: Thou wilt supply all my need according to Thy riches in glory by Christ Jesus.

Praised be Thy holy name, O Lord my God. Amen.

LVII.

THANKSGIVING FOR SPIRITUAL CONSOLATIONS.*

I will extol Thee, O Lord, for Thou hast lifted me up. O Lord my God, I cried unto Thee, and Thou hast healed me. The Lord is my strength and my shield, my heart trusted in Him, and I am helped; therefore my heart greatly rejoiceth, and with my song will I praise Him. Thou hast put gladness in mine heart, even in the time of mine adversity, in the hour of mine anguish. The Lord is my shepherd; I shall not want. He maketh me to lie down in green pastures: He leadeth me beside the still waters. He restoreth my soul: He leadeth me in the paths of righteousness for His name's sake. Yea, though I walk through the valley of the shadow of death, I will fear no evil: for Thou art with me; Thy rod and Thy staff they comfort me. I will praise Thee, O Lord my God, with all my heart, and I will glorify Thy name for evermore, for great is Thy mercy towards me, and Thou hast delivered my soul from the lowest hell. Unless the Lord had been my help, my soul had almost dwelt in silence. When I said my foot slippeth, Thy mercy, O Lord, held me up; in the multitude of my thoughts within me, Thy comforts delight my soul; Thou hast furnished for me a table in the wilderness; Thou hast given me bread from heaven, yea, I have eaten angels' food. Thou hast brought streams also out of the rock; Thou hast made the wilderness a standing water, and dry ground into watersprings. Sing, O Heaven, be joyful, O earth, break forth into singing, O mountains, for the Lord hath comforted His people, and will have mercy upon His afflicted.

I will greatly rejoice in the Lord; my soul shall be joyful in my God, for He hath clothed me with the garments of salvation, He hath covered me with the robe of righteousness.

Praised be Thy name. O Lord my Saviour, the Holy One of Israel, my Redeemer. Amen.

LVIII.

THANKSGIVING FOR SICKNESS.*

O Lord, from whom cometh every good and perfect gift. In great mercy hast Thou afflicted me, to bring me to repentance; Thou hast chastened me by little and little, Thou warnest me by putting me in remembrance wherein I have offended, that leaving my wickedness, I may believe on Thee, O Lord; yet Thou hast remembered my weakness, that I am but flesh, a wind that passeth away and cometh not again. Thou hast not laid upon me more than I can bear.

Blessed be Thy name, O Lord, for all my intervals of ease: Thou hast chastened me right sore, yet Thou hast not given me over to death. As a loving Father, Thou causest me oft to feel Thy rod, that Thou mayest have joy of me in the end; Thou dost scourge and hast mercy; Happy is the man whom Thou correctest. I will not despise the chastening of the Almighty, for He maketh sore and bindeth up, He woundeth and His hands make whole. It is good for me that I have been afflicted, that I might learn Thy statutes. Before I was afflicted I went astray; praised be Thy name, O Lord, for this Thy chastisement, for whom Thou lovest Thou chastenest, and scourgest every son whom Thou dost receive. Let this light affliction, which is but for a moment, work in me a far more exceeding and eternal weight of glory. Lord, Thou hast counted me worthy to suffer with Thee, grant that I may hereafter be glorified with Thee. I thank Thee that by this bondage of sickness Thou hast preserved me from many of the trials and temptations of the world, common to those who are in health, from the danger of being cumbered about much serving; careful and troubled about many things of this world. Thou punishedst me in the sight of men, that my hope may be full of immortality.

Thou triest me as gold in the furnace, receive me, O Lord, as a burnt offering. Sanctify me with Thy Holy Spirit, that laying aside every weight, and the sin that doth so easily beset me, I may run with patience the race that is set before me, looking unto Jesus, the Author and Finisher of our faith, who is set down at the right hand of the throne of God. Praised be His name to all eternity. Amen.

LIX.

THANKSGIVING FOR SORROW.*

I will thank Thee, O Lord and King, and praise Thee, O God my Saviour; for prosperity and adversity, life and death, poverty and riches, come of Thee; all Thy works are good, and Thou wilt give us every needful thing in due season, health and sickness, joy and sorrow, each as we need them. I will sing of Thy power; yea, I will sing aloud of Thy mercy in the morning, for Thou hast been my defence and refuge in the day of my trouble.

Thou dost not afflict willingly, nor grieve the children of men, but Thy desire is to draw us to Thee, that we may walk in the way that leadeth to salvation. Thou sawest, O Lord, that I needed this sorrow, to subdue the imaginations of my heart, to keep me from idols that I might set my affections on things above, not on things of this earth, and lay up for myself treasures in heaven, where moth and rust doth not corrupt, where thieves do not break through and steal. Blessed are they that mourn, for they shall be comforted. Weeping may endure for a night, but joy cometh in the morning. Blessed are they which have been sorrowful for all Thy scourges, for they shall rejoice with Thee, when they have seen all Thy glory, and shall be glad for ever. The Lord hath done great things for me, whereof I am glad; He hath made me to sow in tears, that I might reap in joy; He hath refined me, and chosen me in the furnace of affliction. In a little wrath, He hid His face from me for a moment, but with everlasting kindness He will have mercy on me. I walked on frowardly in the way of mine heart, but Thou wast with me, Lord, to save me. Thou hast corrected me in measure, and hast not left me altogether unpunished. In Thy love Thou dost rebuke me and chasten me.

Blessed be God, even the Father of our Lord Jesus Christ, the Father of all mercies, and the God of all comfort, who comforteth us in all our tribulation. For as the sufferings of Christ abound in us, so our consolation also aboundeth by Christ: To Him be honor, and glory, and praise, and worship, now and evermore. Amen.

LX.

THANKSGIVING FOR OUR BAPTISMAL INHERITANCE.*

Blessed be the God and Father of our Lord Jesus Christ, which, according to His abundant mercy, hath begotten us again unto a lively hope, by the resurrection of Jesus Christ from the dead, to an inheritance incorruptible, and undefiled, and that fadeth not away, reserved in Heaven for those who are kept by the power of God through faith unto salvation. Then shall the righteous shine forth as the sun, in the kingdom of their Father.

I will bless Thy name, O Lord, for I have received the spirit of adoption; Thou hast made me Thine own child; Thine own heir, joint heir with Thy blessed Son, baptized into His body, that glorious Church without spot or wrinkle, or any such thing, holy, and without blemish. I give Thee thanks, O Father, that Thou hast made me meet to be a partaker of the inheritance of the Saints in light, that Thou hast delivered me from the powers of darkness, and hast translated me into the kingdom of Thy dear Son, in whom we have redemption through His blood, even the forgiveness of sins. Blessed be Thy holy name, that Thou hast given me to be a branch of the true vine, a sheep of Thy fold, a part of Thine household, a fellow-citizen with Thy saints, a member of Thy Body; that Thou hast given me a share in Thy promises; in the prayers of Thy children, in the ministry of Thy Holy angels, in the consolations of Thy Holy Spirit. Open mine eyes, O Lord, enlighten mine understanding, that I may know what is the hope of Thy calling, and what is the glory of Thine inheritance in the Saints. Help me, O Lord, holy Father, to make my calling and election sure, that I may walk worthy of Thee, who hast called me unto Thy kingdom and glory.

I bless Thee, O Lord, I praise Thy name for all these inestimable blessings, these consolations in my suffering. How great are Thy mercies, O Lord! The sufferings of this present time are not worthy to be compared to the glory which shall be revealed in us. Eye hath not seen, nor ear heard, neither have entered into the heart of man to conceive the things which Thou hast prepared for them that love Thee.

Praised be Thy name for ever and ever. Amen.

PART II.

PRAYERS FOR THE DYING.

As in Adam all die, so in Christ shall all be made alive.

PRAYERS FOR THE DYING.

I.

IN PROSPECT OF DEATH.

O LORD JESUS CHRIST, who didst suffer death upon the cross, have mercy upon me, for the fear of death hath fallen upon me. I am feeble and sore broken; I have roared for the very disquietness of my heart. Lord, all my desire is before Thee, and my groaning is not hid from Thee; my heart panteth, my strength faileth; as for the light of mine eyes, it is also gone from me. But in Thee, O Lord, do I hope; Thou wilt hear, O Lord my God. Make haste to help me, O God of my salvation. Deliver me from all my transgressions; make me not the reproach of the foolish. O spare me, that I may recover strength before I go hence and be no more seen. Father, if it be possible, let this cup pass from me; nevertheless, not as I will, but as Thou wilt. Yet, O Lord God most holy, O Lord most mighty, O holy and most merciful Saviour, deliver us not into the bitter pains of eternal death. Thou knowest, Lord, the secrets of our hearts. Shut not Thy merciful ears to our prayer; but spare us, Lord most holy. O God most mighty, O holy and most merciful Saviour, Thou most worthy Judge eternal, suffer us not at our last hour, for any pains of death, to fall from Thee. Amen.

II.

FOR THOSE WHO HAVE A FEAR OF DEATH.

O Lord God Almighty, I feel the sentence of death in myself, I know that Thou wilt bring me unto death. All my lifetime I have been subject to bondage through fear of death, and now the terrors of death are fallen upon me. Death is nigh even at my very doors. If I have run with the footmen, and they have wearied me, then how can I contend with horses, if in the land of peace wherein I trusted they wearied me, then what shall I do in the swellings of Jordan? O God, I shall go hence, and not return, even to the land of darkness, and the shadow of death; a land of darkness as darkness itself, and of the shadow of death; without any order, and where the light is as darkness. O Saviour of sinners, it is not the pain I fear, but the enemy cometh on so fast, and I must appear before the judgment-seat to give account of the deeds done in the body, every idle word, and every sin.

Of whom may I seek for succor, but of Thee, O Lord, who for my sins art justly displeased? Yet, O Lord God most holy, O Lord most mighty, O holy and most merciful Saviour, deliver me not into the bitter pains of eternal death.

Thou didst taste death for every man. Help Thou mine unbelief. Save me, Lord, or I perish. Help me to lay hold on the arm of Thy strength.

It was by the suffering of death that Thou didst redeem me. Thou wast partaker of our flesh and blood, that Thou mightest destroy him that hath the power of death, that is, the devil. Thou wilt not leave my soul in hell. Thou wilt show me the path of life. Give me grace to believe that Thou hast abolished death, and hast brought life and immortality to light, and that nothing is able to separate me from Thee, neither life, nor death, nor things present, nor things to come. Thou hast overcome the sharpness of death, and opened the kingdom of heaven to all believers, through Thy precious blood, O Lamb of God. May I believe that although death is passed upon all men, and in Adam I must die, yet in Christ I shall be made alive; that my life is hid with Christ in God, and that in me the saying shall be brought to pass, Death is swallowed up in victory. Thanks be unto God which giveth us the victory through Jesus Christ our Lord. Amen.

III.

WHEN DEATH IS NEAR.

Almighty God, my Heavenly Father, I humbly commend my soul into Thy hands, as into the hands of a faithful Creator, and most merciful Saviour, beseeching Thee that it may be precious in Thy sight.

O Lord Jesus Christ, I cannot say as Thou didst, I have finished the work that Thou hast given me to do, but I thank Thee that Thou hast finished it for me, that Thou hast wrought all Thy works in me.

In me dwelleth no good thing. I am unclean; O Lord, I hear Thy voice, saying, Be ye also ready; I abhor myself, I repent in dust and ashes. How shall I come and appear before the presence of God?

Holy, holy, holy, Lord God Almighty, all my righteousnesses are as filthy rags, they are become abominable.

O Lord, I would not be unclothed, but clothed upon, lest I should be found naked; I cannot buy raiment, my flesh and my heart fail. Miserable, and wretched, and poor, and blind, and naked, I come to Thee. Lord, I believe that the blood of Jesus Christ cleanseth from ALL sin: that from all my filthiness and all my idols He has cleansed me: that He has washed me from my sins in His own blood, and will present me faultless before Thy throne; not for my righteousness, for I was stiff-necked, but to show forth Thy praise, for the glory of Thy name. Into Thy hands I commend my spirit, O Lord God of truth, for Thou hast redeemed me. I have a desire to depart and to be with Christ, which is far better. Lord Jesus, receive my spirit. I am Thine, save me! and receive me, O Father, Son, and Holy Ghost, one God, world without end. Amen.

IV.

FOR THOSE WHO DESIRE TO DEPART, BUT ARE WILLING TO WAIT THE APPOINTED TIME.

O holy, blessed, and glorious Trinity, three persons and one God, have mercy upon me a miserable sinner. My soul longeth, yea, even fainteth, for the courts of the Lord; I have a desire to depart, and to be with Christ, which is far better. In this tabernacle I do groan, being burdened; earnestly desiring to be clothed upon with my house which is from heaven. O Lord, whilst I am at home in the body, I am absent from Thee. I am willing to be absent from the body, and present with the Lord. And yet Thou hast said that to abide in the flesh is more needful for me; and having this confidence, I know that I shall abide and continue until Thou shalt say, Come up hither.

What I shall choose, I wot not. Not as I will, but as Thou wilt: for to me to live is Christ, and to die is gain. I thank Thee, O Father, Lord of heaven and earth, because Thou hast said that to me it is given in the behalf of Christ, not only to believe on Him, but also to suffer for His sake.

O Lord, let this mind be in me, which was also in Christ Jesus. Grant that I may be made perfect through suffering; and if sometimes my soul crieth out, O Lord, how long? let it be Thy pleasure to deliver Thy servant. Jesus, Son of David, have mercy on me, and forgive all my sin.

Lord, I would not live alway. O that I had wings like a dove; for then would I flee away and be at rest. But my times are in Thy hand.

Thou hast appointed unto me a set

time, and wilt remember me; therefore, O Lord, all the days of mine appointed time will I wait till my change come. There is a needs be that I should be in heaviness still; Thou dost purge me thus, that I may bring forth more fruit: I will hope and quietly wait for the salvation of the Lord.

I know, O Lord, that yet a little, and He that shall come will come and will not tarry: and Thou wilt give me grace, though Thou dost tarry, to wait for Thee.

Grant this, O merciful Father, I beseech Thee, to me, and also to all those who long to be at rest; give to us all, patient hearts, and make our wills one with Thy will, through Jesus Christ, our Mediator and Advocate. Amen.

V.

FOR THOSE OF OUR FAMILY AND FRIENDS WHO WILL BE LEFT AT OUR DEATH.

Almighty and everlasting God, I thank and praise Thee for all Thy love to me, and Thy care over me ever since I was born; for all Thy loving-kindness, and tender mercies, for the friends and blessings Thou hast so richly given to me; and for the hope that Thou wilt soon take me hence, that where Thou art, Thy servant may be also.

O my Father, I need not hide anything from Thee, and one thing lies upon my heart, and is often a sore burden; the thought of those that I must leave behind me. Lord, increase my faith. Grant to me that perfect faith, as well as love, which casteth out fear. Give me sure trust and confidence in Thy mercy. If I had none to leave who were so near, and dependent on me, I could gladly die and go to Thee. O Lord, help me to take faster hold of Thy promises, to believe with my whole heart what Thou sayest, Leave Thy fatherless children, and I will preserve them alive, and let your widows trust in me. Like as a father pitieth his children, so Thou wilt pity my children. O teach them from this time to cry unto Thee, my Father, Thou art the guide of my youth. And may the taking away of their earthly father lead them much better to understand what that meaneth, Our Father, which art in heaven. Let them never turn aside from following Thy commandments; or if they wander, O Lord, graciously search and seek them out, and bring them back to the fold; and as they have been baptized into Thy holy name, may they walk as children of the light, and may we meet at last with joy, and not with grief. O Father of mercies, look very graciously upon her whom I must leave, and give her to know, and to feel, that her Maker is her Husband, the Lord of Hosts is His name; and in Thine own good time may she also come up out of the wilderness, leaning on her Beloved. Bless also, O Lord, with Thine own blessing, my [parents], [brothers], and [sisters], and all whom I would mention before Thee. I would remember before Thee our servants, all who have ministered to me, or been kind to me, in my sickness, and throughout my life. If I have enemies, known or unknown, bless them, O Lord. And bless Thy Church here upon earth with unity and godly love. O my Father, hear me: O Jesus, plead Thou for me; O Holy Spirit, make intercession for me, according to the will of God. Amen.

VI.

THE RESURRECTION OF THE BODY—THE GREAT COMFORT IT SHOULD PROVE.

Almighty God, who through Thine only-begotten Son, Jesus Christ our Lord, hast overcome death, and opened unto us the gate of everlasting life, grant that through the grave, the gate of death, we may pass to our joyful resurrection.

O Lord, Thou hast showed me a mystery, that we shall all be changed; that Thou wilt change our vile bodies, and fashion them according to Thy glorious body, that this very body of mine, which day by day becomes more corruptible, shall put on incorruption.

Each day the weakness sinks deeper into me, and is sown in me; and soon this corn of wheat shall fall into the ground and die, and yet it shall be raised in power. O Almighty God, Thy way is past finding out. It is high; I cannot attain unto it; Thou comfortest me with this truth, which I believe with all my heart, though I cannot comprehend it. Lord, what is man, that Thou art mindful of him; or the son of man, that Thou visitest him? I thank Thee, O Father, Lord of heaven and earth, that my body is crumbling away. I thank Thee that it soon must be sown in dishonor, that it may be raised in glory. In this body I have sinned against Thee each day and each hour that I have lived, O Lord. I thank Thee that soon I shall put off this tabernacle, that it will be sown a natural body, to be raised a spiritual body, in which I can never sin against Thee, or grieve Thee any more. Flesh and blood cannot inherit the kingdom of God, neither doth corruption inherit incorruption.

O Lord, I yield my body up to Thee: Thou wilt not let it suffer one pain more than is necessary to lay it in the grave. Although the temple of this body must be taken down before it can be rebuilt and my body must die, yet I know that my Redeemer liveth: and that though after my skin worms destroy this body, yet in my flesh I shall see God, whom I shall see for myself and not another, though my reins be consumed in me; because Christ has risen, and become the first-fruits of them that slept; and He has said that the dead men shall live; together with His dead body shall they arise: and though by man came death, yet by Christ came also the resurrection of the dead. O Lord Jesus, I thank Thee that Thou hast taken away the sting of death, and that Thou hast overcome the sharpness of death, and opened the kingdom of heaven to all believers. Lord, I believe; help Thou mine unbelief. Thou hast made me glad, and my flesh shall rest in hope; not for any righteousness of mine, O Lord, for I have sinned, and come short of Thy glory; but thanks be to God, which giveth us the victory through Jesus Christ our Lord.

My Father, I will praise Thee with my whole heart because Thou hast given me this blessed and holy comfort; I pray Thee to grant the same comfort and hope to all who are sick or dying. May they be able to look forward in hope, and to give thanks because their bodies will be committed to the ground, earth to earth, ashes to ashes, dust to dust, in sure and certain hope of the resurrection to eternal life, through our Lord Jesus Christ.

Grant this, we beseech Thee, O merciful Father, through Jesus Christ, our Mediator and Redeemer. Amen.

VII.

THANKSGIVING FOR DEATH.*

O Lord, life and death are in Thy hands, Thou didst die and hast risen again, that Thou mightest be Lord of the dead and of the living.

Blessed be Thy Name, O Lord my God, for out of judgment hast Thou brought forth mercy; out of a curse hast Thou brought forth a blessing. Thou makest death acceptable unto the needy, and unto him whose strength faileth. The weak look unto Thee, Thou givest them rest; Thou hearest the cry of the afflicted, and dost not prolong their sufferings, for their life is full of trouble.

The righteous is taken away from the evil to come; he shall enter into peace. For blessed are the dead which die in the Lord, they rest from their labors, and their works do follow them.

O Lord Jesus Christ, my Saviour, my Redeemer, Thou hast sanctified death and the grave. Thou hast taken away the curse of death, and made it the gate of immortality; for Thou hast subdued death, and put it under Thy feet. Thou hast risen from the dead, and become the first-fruits of them that slept. O death, where is thy sting? O grave where is thy victory? Thanks be to God who giveth us the victory, through our Lord Jesus Christ. I will thank Thee, O Lord my Saviour, I will bless Thy name for ever. I will thank Thee for my life and for my death; for my joy and for my sorrow, for my health and for my sickness. Praised be Thy name, who livest and reignest with the Father, the King of kings, and Lord of lords, who only hath immortality, dwelling in the light which no man can approach unto; whom no man hath seen, nor can see: to whom be honor and power everlasting. Amen.

VIII.

THANKSGIVING FOR THE JOYS OF HEAVEN.

O Lord, I will praise Thee: though Thou wast angry with me, Thine anger is turned away, and Thou comfortest me. I will praise Thee, O God, for it is a good thing to sing praises to our God; yea, a joyful and a pleasant thing it is to be thankful. O Lord, Thy love is wonderful, for Thou hast set before us a hope full of immortality, an inheritance incorruptible, undefiled, which fadeth not away, reserved in heaven for those who are kept by Thy power, through faith unto salvation. Teach me, O Lord, how to praise Thee, for I cannot order my speech before Thee, by reason of darkness. According to Thine abundant mercy, Thou hast begotten us again unto a lively hope, by the resurrection of our Lord Jesus Christ, whom having not seen we love, in whom, though now we see

Him not, yet believing, we rejoice with joy unspeakable, and full of glory, receiving the end of our faith, even the salvation of our souls. Eye hath not seen, nor ear heard, neither have entered into the heart of man the things which Thou hast prepared for them that love Thee. O Lord, it doth not yet appear what we shall be; but we know that, when He shall appear, we shall be like Him, for we shall see Him as He is, and so shall we ever be with the Lord.

I give Thee hearty thanks, O my Father, that Thou hast revealed to us, that there remaineth a rest for Thy people, and that Jesus is gone to prepare a place for us. Whilst I am in this tabernacle, I am wearied with the burden of my sin, but there shall be no sin there. O Lord, how wonderful to be freed from sin! that even I, who am sore let and hindered in running the heavenly race, shall one day be faultless before Thy throne, without fear of sinning, or of grieving Thee any more, for Thou hast said, there shall be no more curse. In Thy love to my soul, Thou hast chastened me with strong pain here, but there shall be no more pain there. Wearisome nights Thou hast appointed me here, but there shall be no night there, nothing shall enter in that defileth; sorrow and sighing shall flee away. The inhabitant shall no more say, I am sick; the eyes of the blind shall be opened, and the ears of the deaf shall be unstopped, the lame man shall leap as an hart, and the tongue of the dumb shall sing. Help me, O Lord, having this hope, to purify myself, even as Thou art pure, before Thou dost take me to that way of holiness.

O my Father! in Thy house are many mansions; I praise and bless Thee for the hope, that there I shall meet again so many of those whom I have loved on earth, and that we shall go no more out, for there shall be no more death, neither sorrow, nor crying: Thou wilt wipe away tears from off all faces, and they shall hunger no more, nor thirst any more.

Thou hast taught me to believe in the Communion of Saints, and that we are all members of one body: how joyful it is to think of that multitude which no man can number, of all nations, and kindreds, and people, and tongues; who have come out of great tribulation, and have washed their robes, and made them white in the blood of the Lamb, therefore are they before the Throne of God.

O Lord, my flesh is weak, and I am soon weary of serving Thee here, but there they shall serve Thee day and night in Thy temple. These things are faithful and true. Lord, I believe, help Thou my unbelief; and when it pleaseth Thee, may I enter into that rest, and join that multitude in saying, Blessing, and glory, and wisdom, and thanksgiving, and honor, and power, be unto our God, for ever and ever. Amen.

PRAYERS

SUITABLE TO BE READ TO PERSONS IN THEIR LAST HOURS.

FROM THE SERVICE FOR THE VISITATION OF THE SICK.

The short Litany.

The third Collect, O most merciful God.

Verses (occasionally and very slowly repeated) from the cxxx. Psalm.

O Saviour of the world, &c.

The Almighty Lord, who is a most strong tower, &c.

Unto God's gracious mercy we commit thee, &c.

Prayer for a sick child.

Prayer when there appeareth small hope of recovery.

Commendatory prayer.

FROM THE BURIAL SERVICE.

The three verses at the beginning.

The four sentences which begin, Man that is born of a woman, &c.

Second Prayer.

COLLECTS.

For Advent Sunday.

For Sixth Sunday after The Epiphany,

For Easter Even.

For Easter Day.

For Ascension Day.

For Sunday after Ascension Day.

For Sixth Sunday after Trinity.

For Eleventh Sunday after Trinity.

For Twenty-fourth Sunday after Trinity.

For The Annunciation.

For St. Michael's Day.

For All Saints' Day.

After the Communion Service, Assist us mercifully, O Lord, &c.

The two sentences from the Litany, beginning, " By Thine agony," &c., and, " In all time of our tribulation."

Also the versicles beginning, " From our enemies defend us, O Christ."

And the prayer following, " We humbly beseech Thee."

Or some of the following sentences* may be said.

By Thy faintness and exhaustion,
By Thy hours of weakness,
By Thy long hours of woe,
By Thy enduring to the end,
By Thy death of exhaustion,
When laid upon a bed of death,
  Blessed Jesus, deliver us.
By Thy fevered frame,
By Thy parched lips,
By Thine aching brow,
By Thy failing strength,

---

* Selected from " Meditations, and a Litany for each Day in Lent."

By Thy looking for death,
By Thy victory at last,
    Blessed Jesus, deliver us.
By Thy submission to infirmities,
By Thy prayer of humiliation,
By Thy willingness to bear the Cross,
By Thy ever ready succor,
By Thy determination to bear all,
By Thy power to forgive,
    Blessed Jesus, deliver us.
By Thine uncomplaining endurance,
By Thy holy resignation,
By Thy patient waiting,
By Thy footsteps which mark the way,
By Thine unchanging love,
    Blessed Jesus, deliver us,
By Thy going before us,
By Thy knowledge of our trial,
By Thy bitter agony,
By Thine unknown sufferings,
By Thy patient endurance to the end,
By the love that conquered all for us,
    Blessed Jesus, deliver us,
By Thy bursting the chains of death,
By Thy descent into the grave,

By Thy victory over the grave,
By the way thus opened for us,
By the sting of death overcome,
By Thy glorious resurrection,
Most merciful Jesus, save and deliver us.

Jesus, my Saviour! My Redeemer!
Forgive me. Cleanse me. Save me.
Give me patience. Give me strength. Give me peace.
Keep me in life. Keep me in death. Keep me in eternity. Through Thy precious blood,
   O Lamb of God.

TEXTS.

SUITED TO BE READ TO DYING PERSONS.

They should be said *very* slowly, *very* distinctly, and with pauses between; longer or shorter, according to the state of the person.

FOR THOSE WHO ARE TROUBLED IN MIND AND AFRAID LEST THEY SHOULD COME SHORT OF THAT REST.

Remember not the sins of my youth, nor my transgressions: according to Thy mercy remember Thou me for Thy goodness' sake, O Lord. (Ps. xxv. 7.) He is near that justifieth me; who will contend with me? let us stand together: who is mine adversary? let him come near to me. Behold the Lord God will help me; who is he that shall condemn me? (Isa. l. 8, 9.) Thou shalt answer for me, O Lord my God. (Ps. xxxviii. 15. P. B.) Come unto me, all ye that labor and are heavy laden, and I will give you rest. Take my yoke upon you, and learn of me, for I am meek, and lowly in heart, and ye shall find rest unto your souls. For my yoke is easy, and my burden is light. (Matt. xi. 28–30.)

Ps. xxvii. 15, 16. Ps. lxviii. 18. Ps. lxix. 6. Ps. xc. 13–15. Ps. ciii. 8–13. Ps. cvii. 10, 12, 39. Ps. cxxvi. 4–6. Ps.

cxxx. all. Ps. cxlvii. 3. (p. b.) Isa. liv. 7, 8. Isa. lix. 1. Isa. lxi. 1, 3. Jer. xiv. 8, 9. Jer. xxxiii. 6. Lam. iii. 22–27. 32. Dan. ix. 9. Mal. iii. 6. Matt. vii. 8. Matt. viii. 25, 26. Matt. x. 29–31. Phil. i. 6. Heb. v. 7. Heb. vi. 19. Heb. vii. 25. 1 John i. 8, 9. Rev. xxii. 17.

CHRIST JESUS RECEIVES AND PARDONS ALL SINNERS WHO COME TO HIM.

Thou shalt call His name Jesus, for He shall save His people from their sins. (Matt. i. 21.)

God so loved the world, that He gave His only begotten Son, that whosoever believeth in Him should not perish, but have everlasting life. (John iii. 16.)

The blood of Jesus Christ His Son cleanseth us from all sin. (1 John i. 7.)

Him that God exalteth with His right hand to be a Prince and a Saviour, for to give repentance to Israel, and forgiveness of sins. (Acts v. 31.)

Ps. ciii. 3. Ps. cvii. 2. Ps. cxlv. 8, 9. Matt. vii. 7. Matt. xviii. 11. Matt.

xxviii. 18. Luke i. 68. Luke ii. 10, 11, 14. Luke v. 20. Luke xv. 7. Luke xxiii. 42, 43. John i. 29. John vii. 37. John xii. 32. Acts xxvi. 18. 23. Rom. v. 6, 8, 9. Eph. i. 7. 1 Tim. i. 15. Heb. ix. 14. 1 Pet. i. 18, 19. 1 Pet. ii. 24.

THE LOVE OF CHRIST.

The love of Christ constraineth us, because we thus judge, that if one died for all, then were all dead. (2 Cor. v. 14.)

Greater love hath no man than this, that a man lay down his life for his friends. (John xv. 13.)

Unto Him that loved us, and washed us from our sins in His own blood. (Rev. i. 5.)

I am the good Shepherd. The good Shepherd giveth His life for the sheep. (John x. 11.)

Luke xxiii. 34. John iv. 14. John vii. 37, 38. John x. 1. 21. John xiv. 13. John xv. 9–13. 2 Cor. viii. 9. Eph. ii. 4, 5. 7. Eph. ii. 13, 14. 16.

Eph. iii. 14–19. Phil. ii. 5, 6. 8, 9, 10, 11. Coloss. i. 21, 22. 24. 2 Thess. ii. 16. Heb. ii. 10. 17. 1 John iii. 1. Rev. i. 5.

FOR THOSE WHO ARE RESTING IN GOD AND AT PEACE.

God is our refuge and strength, a very present help in trouble. (Ps. xlvi. 1.)

Great is the peace that they have who love Thy law. (Ps. cxix. 165.)

There is therefore now no condemnation to them which are in Christ Jesus, who walk not after the flesh, but after the Spirit. (Rom. viii. 1.)

Ye have need of patience, that, after ye have done the will of God, ye might receive the promise. (Heb. x. 36.)

Deut. xxxii. 4. Deut. xxxiii. 26, 27. 29. Ps. xxxiii. 19. (p. b.) Ps. lv. 22. Ps. lxxxiv. 11, 12. Ps. xci. 1–4. 9. Ps. cxvi. 7, 8. Ps. cxix. 20. Ps. cxxi. 1–5. Ps. cxxxi. all. Isa. xii. 2. Isa. xxvi. 3,

4. Isa. xxxiii. 24. Isa. xlviii. 10. Isa. xlix. 13. Mal. iv. 2. John iv. 14. John xv. 4, 5. 8. Rom. v. i. Rom. viii. 17, 18. 24–32. 1 Cor. iii. 21–23. Eph. ii. 14–20. Eph. vi. 10–17. Phil. iv. 13. 19. Col. i. 11–14. Heb. ix. 14. 28. Heb. xii. 1–12. James i. 2. 1 Pet. i. 7, 8. 1 Pet. v. 6, 7. 10. 2 Pet. i. 11.

WHEN DEATH IS VERY NEAR.

He shall drink of the brook in the way, therefore shall He lift up the head. (Ps. cx. 7.)

He will swallow up death in victory, and the Lord God will wipe away tears from off all faces, and the rebuke of His people shall He take away from off all the earth, for the Lord hath spoken it. (Isa. xxv. 8.)

I am the Resurrection and the Life. (John xi. 25.)

Who shall change our vile body, that it may be fashioned like unto His glorious body, according to the working whereby He is able even to subdue all things unto Himself. (Phil. iii. 21.)

Deut. ix. i. Josh. xxiii. 14. Ps. xvi. 9–11. Ps. xvii. 15. Ps. xxiii. all. Ps. xxxi. 5. 15. Ps. xlviii. 14. Ps. lxxiii. 23–26. Ps. cxvi. 15. Ps. cxliii. 2. Isa. xxxiii. 17. Isa. xliii. 1–3. Hos. xiii. 14. Matt. xxvi. 39. Luke ii. 29, 30. Luke xx. 37, 38. Luke xxii. 44. John v. 21. 25. John vi. 48–51. John xii. 27. John xiv. 1–3. 27. John xvii. 24. Acts vii. 59. Rom. viii. 18. 33–35. 37–39. Rom. xvi. 20. 1 Cor. xiii. 12. 1 Cor. xv. 20. 22. 26. 42. 52. 53–55. 57. 2 Cor. iii. 18. 2 Cor. iv. 10. 16–18. 2 Cor. v. 1–8. Gal. ii. 20. Phil. i. 21. Phil. ii. 8. Col. iii. 1. 3, 4. 1 Thess. iv. 14. 1 Tim. vi. 16. 2 Tim. iv. 8. Tit. ii. 13. Heb. xii. 22–24. Heb. xiii. 14. 1 Pet. i. 3–5. Rev. i. 18. Rev. iii. 11, 12. 20. Rev. xiv. 13.

HEAVEN.

The redeemed of the Lord shall return and come with singing unto Zion, and everlasting joy shall be upon their head; they shall obtain gladness and joy, and sorrow and mourning shall flee away. (Isa. li. 11.)

The sun shall be no more thy light by day; neither for brightness shall the moon give light unto thee: but the Lord shall be unto thee an everlasting light, and thy God thy glory. Thy sun shall no more go down; neither shall thy moon withdraw itself: for the Lord shall be thine everlasting light, and the days of thy mourning shall be ended. (Isa. lx. 19, 20.)

I heard a great voice out of heaven, saying, Behold, the tabernacle of God is with men, and He will dwell with them, and they shall be His people, and God Himself shall be with them, and be their God. And God shall wipe away all tears from their eyes; and there shall be no more death, neither sorrow, nor crying, neither shall there be any more pain: for the former things are passed away. (Rev. xxi. 3, 4.)

Ps. xxxvi. 8, 9. Isa. xxxiii. 21 to end. Isa. xxxv. 5 to end. Rev. v. 9–12. Rev. vii. 9–17. Rev. xii. 10, 11. Rev. xiv. 1–3. Rev. xv. 3, 4. Rev. xix. 9. Rev. xx. 11–13. Rev. xxi. 3–7. 22–27. Rev. xxii. 1–7. 12–14. 20.

THE END.

www.ingramcontent.com/pod-product-compliance
Lightning Source LLC
Chambersburg PA
CBHW031816230426
43669CB00009B/1161